MOMENT FUNCTIONS IN IMAGE ANALYSIS

Theory and Applications

MOMENT FUNCTIONS IN IMAGE ANALYSIS
Theory and Applications

R Mukundan

University Telekom Malaysia

K R Ramakrishnan

Indian Institute of Science

World Scientific

Singapore • New Jersey • London • Hong Kong

Published by

World Scientific Publishing Co. Pte. Ltd.

P O Box 128, Farrer Road, Singapore 912805

USA office: Suite 1B, 1060 Main Street, River Edge, NJ 07661

UK office: 57 Shelton Street, Covent Garden, London WC2H 9HE

British Library Cataloguing-in-Publication Data
A catalogue record for this book is available from the British Library.

MOMENT FUNCTIONS IN IMAGE ANALYSIS: THEORY AND APPLICATIONS

ISBN 981-02-3524-0

This book is printed on acid-free paper.

Printed in Singapore by Uto-Print

To my Mother

                  - Mukundan

To Babaji

                 - Ramakrishnan

Preface

An important field of current research in digital image processing is the representation of image shape features for various applications in recognition, pose recovery and image coding. Several types of image moment functions have been reported in literature as efficient shape descriptors, each having its own relative merits. This book addresses the theoretical and application oriented aspects of image moments, and is intended to be a reference material for those interested in the areas of computer vision and image analysis.

The first part of this book discusses the mathematical properties of geometric, complex and orthogonal moments, while the second part provides an overview of the applications of moments in pattern recognition, object identification, and object pose estimation. A comprehensive list of references is given in bibliography, to help the readers pursue the subject matter in greater depth. The work presented in this book is expected to aid and stimulate further research in the area of moment based feature representation.

Acknowledgments

The content of this book was derived from my research work at the Indian Institute of Science, Bangalore. I am very grateful to my research supervisors Prof. G. Nath, Prof. A. Chakrabarti, and Dr. N. Ramani for their invaluable guidance and suggestions.

I am indebted to Prof. K.R. Ramakrishnan who has co-authored this work, for his inspiration and guidance at every stage of my research work, and the preparation of this book.

I would like to express my gratitude and heartfelt thanks to Mr. P.S. Goel, and Mr. N.K. Malik for their encouragement and advice throughout the course of this work.

I am also grateful to the President and the management of University Telekom Malaysia, for their support in the publication of this book.

R. Mukundan.

I am grateful to the Indian Institute of Science and the Department of Electrical Engineering for providing a stimulating and supportive academic environment.

K.R. Ramakrishnan.

Contents

Part 2: Moment Functions - Applications

Chapter 1
Introduction

Moment functions have a broad spectrum of applications in image analysis, such as invariant pattern recognition, object classification, pose estimation, image coding and reconstruction. A set of moments computed from a digital image, generally represents global characteristics of the image shape, and provides a lot of information about different types of geometrical features of the image. The feature representation capability of image moments has been widely used in object identification techniques in several areas of computer vision and robotics. Geometric moments were the first ones to be applied to images, as they are computationally very simple. With the progress of research in image processing, many new types of moment functions have been introduced in the recent past, each having its own advantages in specific application areas. For example, moment invariants with respect to image rotation can be easily derived from complex moments. Orthogonal moments, on the other hand, characterize independent features of the image and thus have minimum information redundancy in a set.

The properties of image moments have the following analogies in statistics and mechanics. Moments of orders zero, one, and two of a probability density function represent the total probability, the expectation, and variance respectively. In mechanics, these moments of a spatial distribution of mass give the total mass, the centroid position, and the inertia values respectively. Considering an image as a two-dimensional intensity distribution, the geometric moment functions of the pixel values with respect to their spatial locations in the image, can similarly provide the shape information such as the total image area, the coordinates of the image centroid, and the orientation. These shape characteristics can be further used to construct feature vectors that are invariant with respect to image translation, rotation and scaling. While moments of orders zero up to three are used to represent gross level image features, higher order moments contain finer details about the image and are often more sensitive to image noise.

1.1 General Moment Definition

An image can be thought of as a two-dimensional density distribution $f(x,y)$, where the function value denotes the intensity at the pixel location (x,y). Let ζ denote the image region of the x-y plane, which is the domain of the function $f(x, y)$. A general definition of moment functions Φ_{pq} of order $(p+q)$, of the function $f(x, y)$ can be given as follows:

1

$$\Phi_{pq} = \iint_{\zeta} \Psi_{pq}(x,y)\, f(x, y)\, dx\, dy, \qquad\qquad p, q = 0,1,2,3.... \qquad (1.1)$$

where $\Psi_{pq}(x,y)$ is a continuous function of (x, y) in ζ, known as the *moment weighting kernel* or the *basis set*. The indices p, q usually denote the degrees of the coordinates x, y respectively, as defined inside the function Ψ. For an image, the intensity function $f(x,y)$ is bounded and has compact support in ζ, and therefore the integral given in Eq.(1.1) is finite. It is also implied that the 'total mass' of the distribution given by

$$|f| = \iint_{\zeta} f(x,y)\, dx\, dy, \qquad\qquad\qquad (1.2)$$

is positive.

Variations of the definition given in Eq. (1.1) can be found in literature depending on the type of the basis set used. For example, basis functions of polar coordinates (r, θ) will require re-writing of Eq. (1.1) in terms of polar representation of the image coordinate space, such as

$$\Phi_{pq} = \iint_{\zeta} r^{p+q+1}\Psi_{pq}(\theta)\, f(r, \theta)\, dr\, d\theta, \qquad\qquad p, q = 0,1,2,3.... \qquad (1.3)$$

Orthogonal basis functions which are valid only inside the unit circle, will similarly require scaling of the coordinate space ζ to the region $[-1, 1]$. If ζ is considered as a segment of a complex plane z, then the moment definition can be expressed as a complex integral of the function $f(z)$. In the evaluation of moment functions, the continuous surface integrals are often replaced by a direct summation as a first approximation, with appropriate scale factors for the area elements. More accurate methods for moment computation are discussed in detail under relevant chapters of this book.

1.2 Historical Background

The first significant paper on the application of moments to image analysis was published by Hu [88] in 1962. He used geometric moments to generate a set of invariants which were used for automatic character recognition. Subsequently, the method based on geometric moment invariants was used in pattern recognition by Alt [3] in 1962, ship identification by Smith [190] in 1971, aircraft identification by Dudani [50] in 1977, pattern matching by Dirilten [48] in 1977, and scene matching by Wong [216] in 1978. Sadjadi [172] extended the definition of moments into three dimensions and derived the corresponding invariants. In 1980, Teague [196] introduced orthogonal moments and provided the basic concepts and applications of Legendre moments and Zernike moments. Reddi [160] extended the geometric moments to radial moments and provided a generalized framework for deriving radial and angular invariants, in 1981. A more general notion of complex moments was introduced by Abu-Mostafa [2] in 1984, and he developed methods to derive geometric moment invariants from complex moments, and analyzed their properties in terms of information redundancy and noise sensitivity.

By the year 1985, moment functions had been established as a very useful tool in extracting image shape features, and several hardware implementations of moment computation were attempted. Examples are (i) a parallel mesh moment computer by Reeves [163] in 1982, (ii) an optical system to compute intensity moments by Casasent [26] in 1982, and (iii) the development of a moment generating chip for real-time gray scale video processing by Anderson [4] in 1985. Cyganski and Orr [43] treated moments as contravariant symmetric tensors in 1985, and developed methods for relating affine transformations between image pairs for object identification and orientation determination. New application areas like, template matching by Goshtasby [73] in 1985, and attitude determination by Bamieh [11], in 1985, also emerged as potential uses of moment functions. A major development in the theory of moment functions was the introduction of Fourier-Mellin descriptors by Sheng [180] in 1986, which provided a generalized framework for deriving invariants. Some of the recent advances in the field of moment based image analysis are listed below.

- Reconstruction of moment coded images by Tzannes [204], in 1987.

- Rotation invariant pattern recognition using Zernike moment invariants by Khotanzad [99], in 1988.

- Orientation independent vision techniques by Figueiredo [55], in 1988.

- Applications to image data compression by Bougrenet [20], in 1988.

- Object identification using a neural network and Zernike moment invariants by Khotanzad [97], in 1989.

- Fuzzy quaternion approach to object recognition using Zernike moment invariants by Ngan [142], in 1990.

- The revised fundamental theorem of moment invariants by Reiss [168], in 1991.

- Reconstruction aspects of moment descriptors by Pawlak [146], in 1992.

- Calculation of moment invariants using Hadamard Transform by Fu [62], in 1993.

- Analysis of complex moments in Gabor space and applications to texture segmentation by Bigun [17], in 1994.

- Extraction of shape information from texture using local spectral moments by Super [193], in 1995.

- Development of a moment based method for tomographic reconstruction by Milanfar [134], in 1996.

The list of references given above is very brief, and is intended only to present the large spectrum of key application areas of moment functions. An exhaustive list of references is given in the end of this book.

1.3 About this Book

This book presents a survey of image moment functions, their properties, computational aspects and applications. The purpose of this work is (i) to provide a global view of the utility of moment functions in image analysis, (ii) to serve as a compilation of fundamental concepts and applications of moments reported in literature, and (iii) to aid researchers and academicians in the area of computer vision and image analysis with adequate reference material on moment functions. The book is organized into two parts. The mathematical framework underlying basic theoretical concepts on image moments is presented in Part 1. This includes moment definitions, derivations of important formulae and the description of significant results and algorithms. Several applications of image moments in the field of image analysis, and the description of related algorithms are given in   Part 2.

The first part of this monograph introduces different types of moment functions that are commonly used in image analysis, beginning with a detailed description of geometric moments and their invariant functions (Chapter 2). This chapter also gives numerical algorithms for fast computation of geometric moments of binary images. The concept of complex moments and their properties are presented in Chapter 3. These are moments with complex kernels such as radial, Fourier-Mellin and complex-domain functions. Two important orthogonal moments which have found several applications in image representation are Legendre moments and Zernike moments. The properties of Legendre polynomials, and the algorithms related to the computation of Legendre moments are given in Chapter 4. An introduction of the radial polynomials of Zernike, and the characteristics of the associated moments (Zernike moments and Pseudo-Zernike moments), and Zernike moment invariants are included in Chapter 5. Fast methods to compute Zernike moments of binary and gray-level images are also discussed. The properties of geometric moments when viewed as contravariant symmetric tensors are given in Chapter 6.

The second part of this book describes the main application areas of moment functions in image analysis. The capability of moments to provide shape characteristics of an image has been widely put to use in many pattern recognition applications. Moment based algorithms in pattern recognition are briefly discussed in Chapter 7. Moment invariants have also been used as feature descriptors to identify objects, independent of the translation, rotation and scale factors of the image introduced by the camera view geometry. Object identification and classification methods are also included in Chapter 7. Object pose recovery using image moments has found several applications in computer vision. The problem of estimating the object orientation and position parameters with the help of moments computed from images is detailed in Chapter 8, together with the mathematical derivations leading to the solutions of object pose parameters for various object-camera configurations. Miscellaneous applications of moment functions in image analysis are described in Chapter 9. These include moment based algorithms for edge detection, texture segmentation, image reconstruction, clustering and thresholding.

An exhaustive list of invariant functions of geometric moments is given in Appendix 1. Analytical expressions of geometric and Zernike moments of a general elliptical shape are provided in Appendix 2. The bibliographical list given in the end of this book, contains references primarily on the theory and applications of moment functions, reported in the open literature, and covers most of the important technical journals and conference proceedings in the areas of computer vision, image processing, pattern recognition, optical engineering, and robotics.

The motivation for this work came from the need for a survey and compilation of various aspects of moment functions, considering their potential uses and applications in various realms of computer vision and image analysis. An attempt is made to present all important theoretical and application oriented details on most of the commonly used types of image moments. Due to obvious reasons, every method and theory on moments reported in literature could not be included. Only representative algorithms in primary application areas are discussed in detail. Among the many schemes and diverse moment based techniques developed over the past as well as in recent years, a majority of the work has been referred in bibliography, and fundamental concepts and methods have been outlined in the text.

PART 1

Moment Functions - Theory

Chapter 2
Geometric Moments

Geometric moments are the simplest among moment functions, with the kernel function defined as a product of the pixel coordinates. The main advantage with geometric moments is that image coordinate transformations can be easily expressed and analyzed in terms of the corresponding transformations in the moment space. Functions of geometric moments that are invariant with respect to image plane transformations have found many applications in object identification and object pose estimation. Geometric moment computations on images can be easily performed and implemented, as compared to other moments with complex kernel functions. Geometric moments are also sometimes referred to as *Cartesian moments*, or *regular moments*.

2.1 Definitions and Properties

Geometrical moments are defined with the basis set $\{x^p \, y^q\}$ [see Eq. (1.1)]. The $(p+q)^{\text{th}}$ order two-dimensional geometric moments are denoted by m_{pq}, and can be expressed as

$$m_{pq} = \iint_{\zeta} x^p y^q \, f(x, y) \, dx \, dy, \qquad\qquad p, q = 0,1,2,3.... \qquad\qquad (2.1)$$

where ζ is the region of the pixel space in which the image intensity function $f(x, y)$ is defined. Eq. (2.1) has the form of the projection of the function $f(x,y)$ onto the monomial $x^p \, y^q$. The basis set $\{x^p \, y^q\}$, while complete, is not orthogonal (Weierstrass approximation theorem [40]).

Uniqueness theorem : Assuming that the intensity function $f(x, y)$ is piece-wise continuous and bounded in the region ζ, the moment sequence $\{m_{pq}\}$ is uniquely determined by the intensity function $f(x, y)$, and conversely.

Existence theorem : Assuming that the intensity function $f(x, y)$ is piece-wise continuous and bounded in the region ζ, the moments m_{pq} of all orders exist and are finite.

9

The Fourier transform of the intensity function $f(x, y)$ in two dimensions is called the *characteristic function*, and is given by

$$F(u, v) = \iint_{\zeta} e^{i(ux+vy)} f(x, y) \, dx \, dy, \qquad (2.2)$$

where $i = \sqrt{-1}$, and (u, v) denote the spatial frequency coordinates. Rewriting the exponential term in series, and using the definition of geometric moments, one can derive

$$F(u, v) = \sum_{p=0}^{\infty} \sum_{q=0}^{\infty} \frac{i^{p+q}}{p! \, q!} \, u^p v^q \, m_{pq}. \qquad (2.3)$$

From the above equation, it is easy to find that

$$\left[\frac{\partial^p \partial^q F(u, v)}{\partial u^p \partial v^q} \right]_{u=v=0} = i^{(p+q)} \, m_{pq}. \qquad (2.4)$$

Analogous to characteristic function, the *moment generating function* is defined as

$$M(u, v) = \iint_{\zeta} e^{(ux+vy)} f(x, y) \, dx \, dy, \qquad (2.5)$$

and similar to Eq. (2.4) we have

$$\left[\frac{\partial^p \partial^q M(u, v)}{\partial u^p \partial v^q} \right]_{u=v=0} = m_{pq}. \qquad (2.6)$$

The series expansion of the exponential term inside the integral in Eq. (2.5) gives

$$M(u, v) = \sum_{p=0}^{\infty} \frac{1}{p} \sum_{r=0}^{p} \binom{p}{r} m_{p-r,r} \, u^{p-r} v^r. \qquad (2.7)$$

The above equation shows how the function $M(u, v)$ 'generates' moments of all orders in a series which has spatial frequency coefficients.

2.1.1 *Different Types of Geometric Moments*

Variations in the definition of geometric moments given in Eq. (2.1) can be found in literature, depending on the application area. Some commonly used definitions of different types of geometric moments are given below.

Silhouette moments refer to moments calculated from a binary image. Here, the intensity value f(x, y) takes only two values viz., 0 and 1. The gray-level images are sometimes thresholded to segment the object from the background. The pixels on the object region are assigned a value 1, and that on the background region are assigned a value 0. In this case, the image region ζ consists of only those pixels which correspond to points on the object and have a value 1, and such images are called *silhouette images*.

Boundary moments of an image are computed using only the boundary points of an object. The shape of an object is often represented by its edge contour, and consequently the boundary points are only used in such applications, to minimize data storage space and computation time. In this case, the image region ζ consists of only those pixels which correspond to the boundary points of the object shape. An alternate definition of boundary moments as line integrals along the edge segments was introduced by Chen [33]. He defined the boundary moments of a binary image as

$$m_{pq}^{(b)} = \iint_{c} x^p y^q \, ds, \qquad\qquad p, q = 0,1,2,3....$$

where, $ds = (dx^2 + dy^2)^{\frac{1}{2}}$, and c denotes the edge contour.

Standard moments are the usual geometric moments of images which are normalized with respect to scale, translation, and rotation. Image normalization techniques to derive standard moments are described later in Section 7.2.1. Standard moments have the following properties:

$$m_{00} = 1; \quad m_{10} = m_{01} = m_{11} = 0; \quad m_{20} \geq m_{02} ; \quad m_{30} \geq 0. \tag{2.8}$$

Range moments are the moments computed from range images. The intensity function f(x, y) at a pixel of a range image is a measure of the distance of the corresponding object point with respect to the camera. Usually, for all points on the object in a range image, f(x, y) > 0; and for the background region, f(x, y) ≤ 0.

2.1.2 *Shape Representation Using Moments*

The geometric moments of different orders represent different spatial characteristics of the image intensity distribution. A set of moments can thus form a global shape descriptor of an image. The physical interpretation of some of the geometric moments of an image, is described below.

By definition, the moment of order zero (m_{00}) represents the total intensity of an image. For a silhouette image, this term gives the geometrical area of the image region.

The first-order functions m_{10}, m_{01} provide the intensity moment about the y-axis, and x-axis of the image respectively. The intensity *centroid* (x_0, y_0) is given by

$$x_0 = m_{10} / m_{00} ; \qquad y_0 = m_{01} / m_{00} . \qquad (2.9)$$

For a silhouette image, the point (x_0, y_0) gives the geometrical center of the image region. It is often convenient to evaluate the moments with the origin of the reference system shifted to the intensity centroid of the image. This transformation makes the moment computation independent of the position of the image reference system. The moments computed with respect to the intensity centroid are called *central moments*, and are defined as

$$\mu_{pq} = \iint_{\zeta} (x-x_0)^p (y-y_0)^q \ f(x, y) \ dx \ dy, \qquad p, q = 0,1,2,3.... \qquad (2.10)$$

From the definition of central moments, we have

$$\mu_{00} = m_{00} ; \qquad \mu_{10} = \mu_{01} = 0. \qquad (2.11)$$

The second-order moments are a measure of variance of the image intensity distribution about the origin. The central moments μ_{20}, μ_{02} give the variances about the mean (centroid). The covariance measure is given by μ_{11}.

In mechanics, the radius of gyration of a planar mass distribution about an axis is defined as the distance from the axis to a line where all the mass may be assumed to be concentrated, without any change to the second moment about the axis. We attempt below a similar definition of *radius of gyration* of an image. If $y = c$ denotes the line parallel to the x-axis, which is the radius of gyration of the image about the x-axis, then

$$m_{02} = \iint_{\zeta} c^2 \, f(x, y) \, dx \, dy, \tag{2.12}$$

from which we obtain

$$c = (m_{02} / m_{00})^{\frac{1}{2}}. \tag{2.13}$$

Similarly, the radius of gyration of the image about the y-axis is $(m_{20}/ m_{00})^{\frac{1}{2}}$.

The second-order central moments can also be thought of as the *moments of inertia* of the image about a set of reference axes parallel to the image coordinate axes, and passing through the intensity centroid. The *principal axes of inertia* of the image are defined as the set of two orthogonal lines through the image centroid, which when used as the reference system makes the product of inertia component (μ_{11}) vanish. The moments of inertia (μ_{20}, μ_{02}) of the image about this reference system are then called the *principal moments of inertia* of the image. If $\mu_{20}, \mu_{02}, \mu_{11}$ are the second-order central moments of an image in its actual image reference frame, and if I_1, I_2 refer to its principal moment of inertia values, then

$$I_1 = \frac{(\mu_{20} + \mu_{02}) + \left[(\mu_{20} - \mu_{02})^2 + 4\mu_{11}^2\right]^{1/2}}{2},$$

$$I_2 = \frac{(\mu_{20} + \mu_{02}) - \left[(\mu_{20} - \mu_{02})^2 + 4\mu_{11}^2\right]^{1/2}}{2}. \tag{2.14}$$

Note that if $\mu_{11} = 0$, then $I_1 = \mu_{20}$, and $I_2 = \mu_{02}$. The orientation angle θ of one of the principal axis of inertia with the x-axis is given by the following equation:

$$\mu_{11} \tan^2\theta + (\mu_{20} - \mu_{02}) \tan\theta - \mu_{11} = 0.$$

Hence,

$$\theta = \frac{1}{2} \tan^{-1}\left(\frac{2\mu_{11}}{\mu_{20} - \mu_{02}}\right). \tag{2.15}$$

Eqs. (2.14), (2.15) can be used to define an *image ellipse* which has the same moments of inertia and principal axes direction as the original image (Fig.2.1). The lengths a, b of the semi-major axis and semi-minor axis of the image ellipse are given by

$$a = 2 (I_1 / \mu_{00})^{\frac{1}{2}} \; ; \qquad\qquad b = 2 (I_2 / \mu_{00})^{\frac{1}{2}} . \qquad\qquad (2.16)$$

The image ellipse also has a uniform intensity value k inside and zero outside, preserving the value of the zero order moment, i.e.,

$$k = \mu_{00} / (\pi a b). \qquad\qquad (2.17)$$

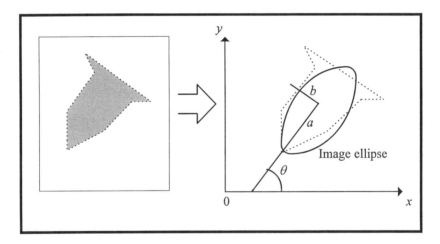

Fig. 2.1 An image and the corresponding image ellipse.

An image ellipse can therefore characterize the fundamental shape features, and also represent the two-dimensional position and orientation. The term $(I_1+I_2)/m_{00}^2$ is sometimes called the shape's *spreadness*, and the term $(I_2-I_1)/(I_1+I_2)$ is called the shape's *elongation*. The parameters a, b, θ as obtained from Eqs. (2.15), (2.16) are called the *elliptical shape descriptors* of the image. Analytical expressions for the geometric moments of a general ellipse are given in Appendix 2.

The third-order moments μ_{30}, μ_{03} denote *skewness* of the image projections. Skewness is a statistical measure of the degree of deviation from symmetry about the mean. If an image is symmetrical about the line $x = x_0$, then $\mu_{30} = 0$. We can therefore consider μ_{30} as a measure of departure from symmetry about the mean axis $x = x_0$. Since μ_{20} is always positive, we can divide the μ_{30} by the term $(\mu_{20})^{3/2}$ to get a non-dimensional quantity. Thus the coefficients of skewness of an image about the x-axis and y-axis are

$$S_x = \mu_{30} / (\mu_{20})^{3/2},$$

$$S_y = \mu_{03} / (\mu_{02})^{3/2}. \tag{2.18}$$

The fourth-order moments μ_{40}, μ_{04} denote *kurtosis* of an image. In statistics, kurtosis is a measure of the flatness or peakedness of a curve. For an image, the corresponding property of the intensity distribution along the x-axis can be defined by the dimensionless quantity $\mu_{40} / (\mu_{20})^2$. For a normal distribution, this quantity has the value 3. Usually a measure of kurtosis over the normal distribution is used. Thus the coefficients of kurtosis about the x-axis and y-axis are defined as

$$K_x = (\mu_{40} / \mu_{20}^2) - 3,$$

$$K_y = (\mu_{04} / \mu_{02}^2) - 3. \tag{2.19}$$

The above discussion shows how geometric moments of different orders characterize different features of an image shape. In several applications, it is further required to have a unique set of shape descriptors which are invariant with respect to image transformations such as scale variation, translation and rotation. The invariant shape features will therefore represent one particular view of an object, irrespective of the distance between the camera and the object, as well as the pan and roll angles of the camera. The next section describes the invariant functions of geometric moments.

2.2 Geometric Moment Invariants

Functions of geometric moments which are invariant with respect to image-plane transformations are used in object identification and pattern recognition applications. For example, in the area of optical character recognition, a set of shape features computed for a character must be capable of identifying the same character with possibly a different size and orientation. Moment invariants constitute one such set of descriptors which can be used under affine transformations of an image.

Consider the following linear transformation of the image coordinates from (x, y) to (x', y'):

$$\begin{bmatrix} x' \\ y' \end{bmatrix} = \begin{bmatrix} a_{11} & a_{12} \\ a_{21} & a_{22} \end{bmatrix} \begin{bmatrix} x \\ y \end{bmatrix} \tag{2.20}$$

where a_{ij}'s are constants and $|a_{11} a_{22} - a_{12} a_{21}| \neq 0$.

The geometric moments m'_{pq} of the transformed image $f'(x,y)$ are given by

$$m'_{pq} = \iint\limits_{\zeta} (x')^p (y')^q f'(x', y') \, dx' \, dy', \qquad\qquad p, q = 0,1,2,3....$$

$$= \iint\limits_{\zeta} (a_{11}x + a_{12}y)^p (a_{21}x + a_{22}y)^q f(x, y) \, \Delta \, dx \, dy, \tag{2.21}$$

where $\Delta = a_{11}a_{22} - a_{21}a_{12}$ is the determinant of the transformation matrix. We have also assumed in the above derivation that the image intensity values are preserved during the transformation, i.e., $f(x, y) = f'(x', y')$. The integral in Eq. (2.21) can be expanded into a series of moments m_{pq} of the initial image, to obtain the equation relating moments of the initial and transformed images. The moment equations thus derived for different orders, can be algebraically manipulated to eliminate the image transformation parameters a_{ij}, to yield *invariant* expressions in moment functions.

2.2.1 *Translation and Scale Invariants*

The central moments given in Eq. (2.10) are translation invariant, by definition. This is due to the fact that the image centroid (x_0, y_0) moves with the image under translation, and the central moments are defined with respect to this point as the origin. Analytical expressions useful in computing second and third order central moments directly from ordinary geometric moments are given below.

$\mu_{02} = m_{02} - y_0 \, m_{01}$

$\mu_{20} = m_{20} - x_0 \, m_{10}$

$\mu_{11} = m_{11} - y_0 \, m_{10}$

$\mu_{30} = m_{30} - 3 \, x_0 \, m_{20} + 2 \, x_0^2 \, m_{10}$

$\mu_{03} = m_{03} - 3 \, y_0 \, m_{02} + 2 \, y_0^2 \, m_{01}$

$$\mu_{21} = m_{21} - 2 \, x_0 \, m_{11} - y_0 \, m_{20} + 2 \, x_0^2 \, m_{01}$$

$$\mu_{12} = m_{12} - 2 \, y_0 \, m_{11} - x_0 \, m_{02} + 2 \, y_0^2 \, m_{10} \tag{2.22}$$

A transformation of the image pixel coordinates by a uniform scale factor k, is given by

$$x' = k \, x ; \qquad y' = k \, y. \tag{2.23}$$

The above transformation also leads to the following expression for the scaled area element:

$$dx' \, dy' = k^2 \, dx \, dy. \tag{2.24}$$

The moments of the scaled image can now be expressed in terms of the moments of the original image as

$$m_{pq}' = k^{p+q+2} \, m_{pq} . \tag{2.25}$$

From the above equation we also get

$$m_{00}' = k^2 \, m_{00}. \tag{2.26}$$

Eliminating the unknown scale factor k from the above two equations, we get

$$\frac{m_{pq}'}{(m_{00}')^{(p+q+2)/2}} = \frac{m_{pq}}{(m_{00})^{(p+q+2)/2}}. \tag{2.27}$$

Thus, we see that the term η_{pq} defined by

$$\eta_{pq} = \mu_{pq} / (\mu_{00})^{(p+q+2)/2} \tag{2.28}$$

is invariant under both translation and scale variation of an image. Scale invariance can also be alternatively achieved by any of the following *scale-normalization* schemes [14], [155]:

$$\eta_{pq} = \mu_{pq} / (\mu_{20} + \mu_{02})^{(p+q+2)/4} ,$$

$$\eta_{pq} = \frac{\mu_{pq}}{\mu_{00}} \left(\frac{\mu_{00}}{\mu_{20} + \mu_{02}} \right)^{(p+q)/2} \tag{2.29}$$

If an image is transformed with unequal scale factors k_1, k_2 along x and y axes respectively, then the transformed moments can be obtained as

$$m_{pq}' = (k_1)^{p+1} (k_2)^{q+1} m_{pq}. \tag{2.30}$$

Writing the explicit equations for the first few orders of the moments, and eliminating k_1, k_2 from these equations, we can find that the term

$$\eta_{pq} = \frac{(\mu_{00})^{(p+q+2)/2}}{(\mu_{20})^{(p+1)/2} (\mu_{02})^{(q+1)/2}} \mu_{pq} \tag{2.31}$$

is invariant with respect non-uniform scaling of the image [143]. Such invariants are called *aspect ratio invariants*.

2.2.2   Rotation Invariants

A rotation of an image by an angle θ has an associated pixel coordinate transformation given by

$$\begin{bmatrix} x' \\ y' \end{bmatrix} = \begin{bmatrix} \cos\theta & -\sin\theta \\ \sin\theta & \cos\theta \end{bmatrix} \begin{bmatrix} x \\ y \end{bmatrix}. \tag{2.32}$$

The corresponding transformations of the moment terms m_{pq} can be analyzed to derive functions of m_{pq} which are independent of the rotation angle θ. For example, the total image intensity moment m_{00} is an invariant under image rotation. The second-order moments of the rotated image can be related to the initial moments of the image by the following equations [see Eq. (2.21)] :

$$m'_{20} = \left(\frac{1+\cos\theta}{2} \right) m_{20} - (\sin 2\theta) m_{11} + \left(\frac{1-\cos\theta}{2} \right) m_{02}$$

$$m'_{11} = \left(\frac{\sin 2\theta}{2} \right) m_{20} + (\cos 2\theta) m_{11} - \left(\frac{\sin 2\theta}{2} \right) m_{02}$$

$$m'_{02} = \left(\frac{1-\cos\theta}{2}\right)m_{20} + (\sin 2\theta)m_{11} + \left(\frac{1+\cos\theta}{2}\right)m_{02} \qquad (2.33)$$

From the above equations, it is easy to see that the term $(m_{20} + m_{02})$ is rotation invariant. The method to derive rotation invariants using the theory of algebraic invariants as proposed by Hu [88], is described later in Section 2.2.4. If we use the terms η_{pq} given in Eq. (2.28), in place of m_{pq} in the expressions for rotation invariants, we get functions that are invariant with respect to translation, scale variation, and rotation of an image. Such invariant functions are called *moment invariants*. A set of second and third order moment invariants is given below.

$$\varphi_1 = \eta_{20} + \eta_{02}$$

$$\varphi_2 = (\eta_{20} - \eta_{02})^2 + 4\eta_{11}^2$$

$$\varphi_3 = \eta_{20}\,\eta_{02} - \eta_{11}^2$$

$$\varphi_4 = (\eta_{30} - 3\eta_{12})^2 + (3\eta_{21} - \eta_{03})^2$$

$$\varphi_5 = (\eta_{30} + \eta_{12})^2 + (\eta_{21} + \eta_{03})^2 \qquad (2.34)$$

An exhaustive list of invariant functions is given in Appendix 1.

2.2.3   *The Fundamental Theorem of Moment Invariants*

The fundamental theorem of moment invariants was first formulated by Hu [88] based on the theory of algebraic invariants, to derive functions of moments which are invariant with respect to affine transformations of images. The mathematical preliminaries needed for proving this theorem are given below.

A homogeneous polynomial of degree p, in two variables u, v can be expressed in the binary form

$$\sum_{r=0}^{p} \binom{p}{r} a_{p-r,\,r}\; u^{p-r}\, v^r\,,$$

where, a_{ij} denote the polynomial coefficients. The above expression can be written in a compact form using *Cayley's notation* as

$$(a_{p0}\,,\; a_{p-1,1}\,,\; a_{p-2,2}\,,\; a_{p-3,3}\,,\; \ldots\ldots\,,\; a_{0p}\,)\; (u,\, v)^p \qquad (2.35)$$

and is known as an *algebraic form* of order p. With the above notation, we can write

$$(ux + vy)^p = (x^p,\ x^{p-1}y,\ x^{p-2}y^2,\ \dots,\ y^p\ )\ (u,\ v)^p$$
$$= (u^p,\ u^{p-1}v,\ u^{p-2}v^2,\ \dots,\ v^p\ )\ (x,\ y)^p. \qquad (2.36)$$

The moment generating function in Eq. (2.7) can be expressed as

$$M(u,\ v) = \sum_{p=0}^{\infty} \frac{1}{p!} (m_{p0},\ m_{p-1,1},\ m_{p-2,2},\ m_{p-3,3},\ \dots,\ m_{0p})\ (u,\ v)^p. \qquad (2.37)$$

Consider a general linear transformation of the variables $(u,\ v)$ to $(u',\ v')$ given by

$$\begin{bmatrix} u \\ v \end{bmatrix} = \begin{bmatrix} k_1 & k_2 \\ k_3 & k_4 \end{bmatrix} \begin{bmatrix} u' \\ v' \end{bmatrix} \qquad (2.38)$$

where k_1, k_2, k_3, k_4 are constants, and $k_1 k_4 - k_2 k_3 \neq 0$. The above transformation induces the following transformation in the algebraic form given in Eq. (2.35):

$$(a_{p0},\ a_{p-1,1},\ a_{p-2,2},\ \dots,\ a_{0p})\ (u,\ v)^p = (a_{p0}',\ a_{p-1,1}',\ a_{p-2,2}',\ \dots,\ a_{0p}')\ (u',\ v')^p \qquad (2.39)$$

where a_{ij}' denote the new coefficients after substituting for the variables $u,\ v$. A homogeneous polynomial $I(a)$ of the coefficients a_{ij} is called an *algebraic invariant* of weight w, if

$$I(a_{p0},\ a_{p-1,1},\ \dots,\ a_{0p}) = \Delta^w\ I(a_{p0}',\ a_{p-1,1}',\ \dots,\ a_{0p}'), \qquad (2.40)$$

where $\Delta = k_1 k_4 - k_2 k_3$. The total degree of a term in the homogeneous polynomial $I(a)$ is referred to as the order of the invariant polynomial.

Fundamental theorem of moment invariants : If an algebraic form of order p has an algebraic invariant $I(a)$ of weight w under an affine transformation, then the moments of order p have the same invariant of weight $d+w$, where d is the order of the invariant polynomial.

Proof: Consider the following algebraic form of order p:

$$(m_{p0},\ m_{p-1,1},\ m_{p-2,2},\ m_{p-3,3},\ \dots,\ m_{0p})\ (u,\ v)^p,$$

where the polynomial coefficients m_{ij} are the pth-order moments of an image. A transformation in the variables u, v of the form given in Eq. (2.38) introduces a change in these coefficients to say, a_{ij}', such that

$$(m_{p0}, m_{p-1,1}, m_{p-2,2}, \ldots, m_{0p})\,(u, v)^p = (a_{p0}', a_{p-1,1}', a_{p-2,2}', \ldots, a_{0p}')\,(u', v')^p.$$

(2.41)

Associated with the transformation in Eq. (2.38), we define a corresponding image coordinate transformation $(x, y) \to (x', y')$:

$$\begin{bmatrix} x' \\ y' \end{bmatrix} = \begin{bmatrix} k_1 & k_3 \\ k_2 & k_4 \end{bmatrix} \begin{bmatrix} x \\ y \end{bmatrix}$$

(2.42)

The vectors (u, v) and (x, y) transforming as in Eqs. (2.38) and (2.42) respectively, are called *contragradient* vectors. These vectors have the property

$$ux + vy = u'x' + v'y'.$$

(2.43)

Using the above expression for $ux + vy$ in Eq. (2.5) and noting that

$$dx\,dy = dx'\,dy' / \Delta,$$

(2.44)

where Δ is the determinant of the transformation matrix in Eq. (2.42), we have

$$M(u,v) = M'(u', v') / \Delta,$$

(2.45)

where M' is the moment generating function of the transformed image. Comparing with Eq. (2.37), we get

$$(m_{p0}, m_{p-1,1}, m_{p-2,2}, \ldots, m_{0p})\,(u, v)^p = \left(\frac{m_{p0}'}{\Delta}, \frac{m_{p-1,1}'}{\Delta}, \ldots, \frac{m_{0p}'}{\Delta} \right)(u', v')^p$$

(2.46)

Comparing the above equation with Eq. (2.41), we find that

$$a_{ij} = m_{ij}' / \Delta.$$

(2.47)

If $I(a)$ is an invariant of weight w of the algebraic form in Eq. (2.41), then from the above equation we have

$$I\left(\frac{m_{p0}{}'}{\Delta}, \frac{m_{p-1,1}{}'}{\Delta}, \ldots, \frac{m_{0p}{}'}{\Delta}\right) = \Delta^w \, I(m_{p0}, m_{p-1,1}, m_{p-2,2}, \ldots, m_{0p})$$

$$(2.48)$$

If d is the order of the invariant polynomial I, then

$$(1/\Delta^d) \, I(m_{p0}{}', m_{p-1,1}{}', m_{p-2,2}{}', \ldots, m_{0p}{}') = \Delta^w \, I(m_{p0}, m_{p-1,1}, m_{p-2,2}, \ldots, m_{0p})$$

$$(2.49)$$

which proves the theorem.

2.2.4 Derivation of Invariants Under Image Rotation

The image transformation of the type given in Eq. (2.32) representing an in-plane rotation, always has an orthogonal transformation matrix, so that $\Delta = 1$. From Eq. (2.46) we have

$$(m_{p0}, m_{p-1,1}, m_{p-2,2}, \ldots, m_{0p})(u, v)^p = (m_{p0}{}', m_{p-1,1}{}', m_{p-2,2}{}', \ldots, m_{0p}{}')(u', v')^p$$

$$(2.50)$$

where

$$\begin{bmatrix} u' \\ v' \end{bmatrix} = \begin{bmatrix} \cos\theta & \sin\theta \\ -\sin\theta & \cos\theta \end{bmatrix} \begin{bmatrix} u \\ v \end{bmatrix}$$

$$(2.51)$$

Defining new variables U, V, U', V' as

$$U = (u+iv)/2; \quad V = (u-iv)/2; \quad U' = (u'+iv')/2; \quad V' = (u'-iv')/2,$$

$$(2.52)$$

where $i = \sqrt{-1}$, we get

$$U = U' \, e^{-i\theta}; \qquad V = V' \, e^{i\theta},$$

$$(2.53)$$

and

$$u = U + V; \quad v = i(V - U).$$

$$(2.54)$$

Changing the variables in Eq. (2.50) using the expressions in (2.52),

$$(n_{p0}, n_{p-1,1}, n_{p-2,2}, ..., n_{0p}) (U, V)^p = (n_{p0}', n_{p-1,1}', n_{p-2,2}', ..., n_{0p}') (U', V')^p$$

$$= (n_{p0}', n_{p-1,1}', n_{p-2,2}', ..., n_{0p}') (U\, e^{i\theta}, V\, e^{-i\theta})^p \tag{2.55}$$

where n's are the coefficients which are functions of the old coefficients m. More specifically,

$$n_{p-r,\, r} = \sum_{l=0}^{r} (-1)^l \binom{p-2l}{l} \sum_{k=0}^{r} \binom{r}{k} m_{p-2k-l,\, 2k-l}, \qquad p-2r > 0. \tag{2.56}$$

Equating the coefficients of $U^{p-r} V^r$ on both sides of Eq. (2.55),

$$n_{p-r,r} = e^{i(p-2r)\theta}\, n'_{p-r,r}. \tag{2.57}$$

From the above equation, we can construct the following homogeneous expressions that are independent of θ:

$$n'_{11} = n_{11}$$
$$n'_{20}\, n'_{02} = n_{20}\, n_{02}$$
$$n'_{30}\, n'_{03} = n_{30}\, n_{03} \tag{2.58}$$

The terms in the above equations can be expressed as functions of $m_{p-r,r}$ to obtain the invariant polynomials. For example,

$$n_{20}\, n_{02} = (m_{20} - m_{02})^2 + 4\, m_{11}^2. \tag{2.59}$$

The polynomials obtained by the above procedure are invariants of the algebraic form (2.50) under the transformation (2.51). By the fundamental theorem of moment invariants, these polynomials are indeed invariants of the image transformation (2.32). The commonly used set of rotational invariants are given in Eq. (2.34), and an exhaustive set of invariant polynomials and the corresponding moment invariants can be found in [14], [218], and Appendix 1.

2.2.5 *Contrast and Blur Invariants*

Moment invariants may additionally be required to have contrast invariance property, especially while processing gray-level images. An image which undergoes a uniform contrast variation can be represented equivalently by a scaling of the intensity function. Thus, if $f(x, y)$ denotes the intensity distribution of the original image, and if $f'(x, y)$ denotes the transformed intensity values, then

$$f'(x, y) = k \, f(x, y) \tag{2.60}$$

where, k is the contrast scale factor. The moment invariants given in Eq. (2.34) can be derived for the transformed image as follows:

$$
\begin{aligned}
\varphi_1 &= k \, (\eta_{20} + \eta_{02}) \\
\varphi_2 &= k^2 \, [\, (\eta_{20} - \eta_{02})^2 + 4\eta_{11}^2 \,] \\
\varphi_3 &= k^2 \, [\, \eta_{20} \, \eta_{02}^2 - \eta_{11}^2 \,] \\
\varphi_4 &= k^2 \, [\, (\eta_{30} - 3\eta_{12})^2 + (3\eta_{21} - \eta_{03})^2 \,] \\
\varphi_5 &= k^2 \, [\, (\eta_{30} + \eta_{12})^2 + (\eta_{21} + \eta_{03})^2 \,]
\end{aligned}
\tag{2.61}
$$

By eliminating k from the above equations, we can derive expressions which have all the properties of moment invariants with the additional feature of image contrast invariance. Examples of such functions are (φ_2/φ_1^2), (φ_2/φ_3), and (φ_4/φ_5).

The derivation of invariants with respect to image blur is given [58]. The blurred image $g(x, y)$ is represented as the convolution of the original (ideal) image $f(x, y)$ with a space invariant point-spread function (PSF), $h(x, y)$ as

$$g(x, y) = f(x, y) * h(x, y). \tag{2.62}$$

If μ^f, μ^g, μ^h denote the central moments of the functions $f(x, y)$, $g(x, y)$, $h(x, y)$ respectively, then

$$\mu^g_{pq} = \sum_{i=0}^{p} \sum_{j=0}^{q} \binom{p}{i}\binom{q}{j} \mu^f_{ij} \, \mu^h_{p-i,\,q-j}. \tag{2.63}$$

Assuming that the blur is *symmetric* with respect to both the axes and both the diagonals, and that $\mu^h_{00} = 1$, we have

$$\mu^h_{pq} = \mu^h_{qp}, \quad \text{for all } p, q$$

and $\qquad \mu^h_{pq} = 0, \quad \text{if } p \text{ or } q \text{ is odd.} \tag{2.64}$

From Eq. (2.63) it can be seen that the terms μ^g_{00} , μ^g_{11} , $\mu^g_{20}-\mu^g_{02}$, μ^g_{12}, μ^g_{21}, μ^g_{30}, μ^g_{03} are invariants with respect to symmetric blur. The derivation of higher-order blur invariants are given in [58].

2.3 Fast Computation of Geometric Moments

The expression for moment functions as given in Eq. (2.1) involves continuous integration of the intensity values over the image region. The image, however, consists of only a discrete array of pixel positions, with each pixel containing a quantized gray-level value. The immediate digital approximation of Eq. (2.1) for computing the moments of an NxN image would be

$$m_{pq} = \sum_{x=1}^{N} \sum_{y=1}^{N} x^p y^q f(x, y). \qquad (2.65)$$

The above expression for evaluating the moments of an image is called the *direct sum* method. For a binary image, the intensity function 'f' takes a value '1' for the image region, while a value of '0' represents the background.   In such a case, Eq. (2.65) can be simplified into

$$m_{pq} = \sum \sum x^p y^q, \qquad (2.66)$$

where, x, y are the pixel coordinates such that $f(x, y)=1$. Methods for the fast computation of the moment integral in Eq. (2.1) for a binary image are detailed below.

2.3.1 *The δ - Method*

The δ-Method for computing the moment functions of a binary image using only the boundary points of the image region, was introduced by Zakaria [224]. A binary image defined over a closed convex region ζ can be represented by the set,

$$(<x_{1k}, x_{2k}>, y_k), \quad k = 0,1,2,...n, \qquad (2.67)$$

where, x_{1k}, x_{2k} denote the x-coordinates of the boundary points of the kth image row having an ordinate value y_k .   Among all the image rows, y_0, y_n are respectively the minimum and maximum values of the y-coordinates,   and n denotes the number of image rows in the region (Fig. 2.2).

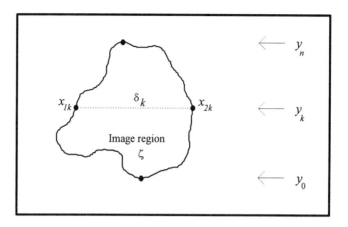

Fig. 2.2 Image region definition in terms of boundary points.

Defining δ_k as the distance between the boundary pixels on the kth row, we have

$$|x_{2k} - x_{1k}| = \delta_k;$$

$$|y_{k+1} - y_k| = 1. \tag{2.68}$$

Eq. (2.66) can now be written as

$$m_{pq} = \sum_{k=1}^{n} (y_k)^q \sum_{i=1}^{\delta_k} (x_{1k} + i)^p. \tag{2.69}$$

The above expression can be easily evaluated for different values of p, and q. For example,

$$m_{0q} = \sum_{k=1}^{n} \delta_k (y_k)^q, \qquad\qquad q=0,1,2,3...$$

$$m_{1q} = \sum_{k=1}^{n} [\delta_k x_{1k} + (\delta_k^2 - \delta_k)/2] (y_k)^q, \qquad\qquad q=0,1,2,3...$$

$$m_{2q} = \sum_{k=1}^{n} [\delta_k x_{1k}^2 + (\delta_k^2 - \delta_k) x_{1k} + (2\delta_k^3 - 3\delta_k^2 + \delta_k)/6] (y_k)^q, \qquad q=0,1,2,3...$$

$$\tag{2.70}$$

As is evident from the above equations, the double summation over each pixel of the image required to evaluate the moment expression in Eq. (2.66), can be reduced to single summations over the boundary points using the factor δ_k. The following result can also be used to further reduce the amount of computation:

$$m_{pq,k} = m_{p0,k}\ y_k^q \tag{2.71}$$

where $m_{pq,k}$ is contribution of the kth row in the moment equation [see Eq. (2.74)]. More expressions for higher order moments can be found in [224].

2.3.2 *The Rectangular Integration Method*

The method of rectangular integration uses the same image representation as in the δ-method, but performs the integration over rectangular regions around the image rows (Fig. 2.3).

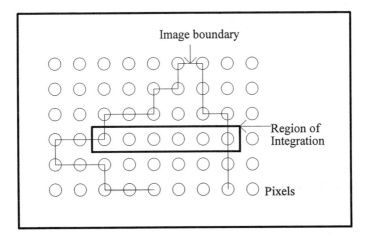

Fig. **2.3** Rectangular integration method.

Each image row as represented in Eq. (2.67) is enclosed in a rectangular region with vertices $(x_{1k}-\frac{1}{2}, y_k-\frac{1}{2})$, $(x_{2k}+\frac{1}{2}, y_k-\frac{1}{2})$, $(x_{2k}+\frac{1}{2}, y_k+\frac{1}{2})$, and $(x_{1k}-\frac{1}{2}, y_k+\frac{1}{2})$. The moment integral is evaluated over each of the above regions, and summed up for the entire image. Denoting the contribution of the kth row to the moment value by $m_{pq,k}$, and evaluating the moment integral over the rectangle around this row, we get

$$m_{pq,k} = \int_{x_{1k}-\frac{1}{2}}^{x_{2k}+\frac{1}{2}} \int_{y_k-\frac{1}{2}}^{y_k+\frac{1}{2}} x^p y^q \, dx \, dy, \qquad p, q = 0,1,2,3.... \tag{2.72}$$

i.e.,

$$m_{pq,k} = \frac{[(x_{2k}+\frac{1}{2})^{p+1} - (x_{1k}-\frac{1}{2})^{p+1}][(y_k+\frac{1}{2})^{q+1} - (y_k-\frac{1}{2})^{q+1}]}{(p+1)(q+1)} \tag{2.73}$$

and

$$m_{pq} = \sum_{k=1}^{n} m_{pq,k} \tag{2.74}$$

Explicit expressions for the first few moments in terms of the boundary points using the above method are given in [45]. A more accurate variation of the above method using *trapezoidal integration* rule can be obtained as follows:

$$m_{pq,k} = \frac{\left(\dfrac{x_{2k} + x_{2,k+1}}{2}\right)^{p+1} - \left(\dfrac{x_{1k} + x_{1,k+1}}{2}\right)^{p+1}}{p+1} \cdot \frac{\left(y_k + \frac{1}{2}\right)^{q+1} - \left(y_k - \frac{1}{2}\right)^{q+1}}{q+1} \tag{2.75}$$

2.3.3 The Contour Integration Method

The contour integration method uses Green's theorem to reduce the two-dimensional surface integral of the moment functions to a single-dimensional contour integral along the boundary points.

Green's theorem: If P, Q are scalar-point functions defined and continuous over a two-dimensional region ζ, then

$$\iint_{\zeta} \left(\frac{\partial Q}{\partial x} - \frac{\partial P}{\partial y} \right) dx \, dy = \int_{C} (P \, dx + Q \, dy), \tag{2.76}$$

where, C is the closed contour edge of the region ζ.

Defining

$$P = 0; \qquad Q = \frac{x^{p+1}y^q}{p+1}, \qquad (2.77)$$

and comparing with the moment integral, we get

$$m_{pq} = \frac{1}{p+1} \int_C x^{p+1}y^q \, dy . \qquad (2.78)$$

We give below three different methods to evaluate the above integral, depending on different representations of the image boundary.

(1). When the image boundary is given in terms of the pixel coordinates of the end-points of each image row as in Eq. (2.67), the integral in (2.78) can be evaluated using the *mean-value theorem* on integrals along linear segments on the boundary connecting consecutive end-points of the image rows. The final result after adding up the components of all the rows is given below.

$$m_{pq} = \sum_{k=0}^{n-1} \frac{\left(x_{2k}^{p+1} - x_{1k}^{p+1}\right)y_k^q + \left(x_{2(k+1)}^{p+1} - x_{1(k+1)}^{p+1}\right)y_{k+1}^q}{2(p+1)} . \qquad (2.79)$$

(2). When the image boundary is represented by a polygon of n vertices, and the pixel coordinates of the vertices are given as (x_i, y_i), $i=1,...n$, then by applying the mean-value theorem on integrals along the linear segments of the edge polygon, we get [175]

$$m_{pq} = \frac{1}{(p+1)} \sum_{i=1}^{n} \left(\frac{x_{i+1} + x_i}{2}\right)^{p+1} \left(\frac{y_{i+1} + y_i}{2}\right)^{q+1} \left(y_{i+1} - y_i\right). \qquad (2.80)$$

(3). When the image boundary is represented by a polygon of n vertices, and the equation of each polygonal line segment is given as $y = y_i + a_i (x - x_i)$, $i = 1,2,....n$, where a_i is the slope of the ith line segment, then by substitution in Eq. (2.78) we get [94],[13]

$$m_{pq} = \sum_{i=1}^{n} \left(\frac{a_i}{p+1}\right) \sum_{k=0}^{q} \binom{q}{k} \frac{a_i^k (y_i - a_i x_i)^{q-k} (x_{i+1}^{p+k+2} - x_i^{p+k+2})}{p+k+2} . \qquad (2.81)$$

Since we consider a closed polygon, we also have $x_{n+1} = x_1$, and $y_{n+1} = y_1$. If the ith line is vertical, its slope a_i is not defined. In such a case, the contribution D_i due to this line segment can be redefined as

$$D_i = \frac{x_i^{p+1}(y_{i+1}^{q+1} - y_i^{q+1})}{(p+1)(q+1)} . \tag{2.82}$$

2.3.4 Comparison of Numerical Methods

This section gives a comparative analysis of the numerical methods for moment computation discussed above. An ellipse is used as a test image, with semi-major axis length a=30 pixels, and semi-minor axis length b=20 pixels. The image is then rotated anti-clockwise by an angle of 45 degrees, and translated to coincide the center of the ellipse with the pixel position given by x_0=10, y_0=30. The exact values of moments of this shape can be analytically obtained as follows: (Analytical expressions for the moments of a general ellipse are given in Appendix 2.)

$$m_{00} = \pi \, ab$$

$$m_{10} = \pi \, ab \, x_0 ; \quad m_{01} = \pi \, ab \, y_0$$

$$m_{20} = \pi \, ab \, [\, x_0^2 + (a^2 + b^2)/8 \,]$$

$$m_{02} = \pi \, ab \, [\, y_0^2 + (a^2 + b^2)/8 \,]$$

$$m_{11} = \pi \, ab \, [\, x_0 y_0 + (a^2 - b^2)/8 \,]. \tag{2.83}$$

The above set of moments were evaluated for the ellipse image on a 64x64 pixel grid using the following methods described in the previous sections:

Method-1 :   The δ- method using Eq. (2.70).
Method-2 :   The rectangular integration method using Eq. (2.73).
Method-3 :   The trapezoidal integration method using Eq. (2.75).
Method-4 :   The contour integration method using Eq. (2.79).

The average percentage error (ε) in the computed moments is calculated as

$$\varepsilon = \frac{1}{6} \sum_{p=0}^{2} \sum_{q=0}^{2} \frac{|m_{pq}^{computed} - m_{pq}^{exact}| \, 100}{m_{pq}^{exact}} . \tag{2.84}$$

The computed moment values and the average percentage of error are tabulated in Table 2.1.

	Exact value	Method-1	Method-2	Method-3	Method-4
m_{00}	1884.96	1878.00	1929.00	1857.00	1869.00
m_{10}	18849.56	17841.00	19290.00	18657.50	18690.00
m_{01}	56548.67	56340.00	57870.00	55056.00	56070.00
m_{20}	494800.84	472419.00	516768.75	482495.50	489113.00
m_{02}	2002765.25	1994596.00	2051706.88	1933136.75	1980871.00
m_{11}	683296.38	651180.00	698866.00	668597.00	674512.50
ε (%)	-	2.62	2.70	2.21	1.01

Table 2.1 Comparison of the accuracy of moments using different methods.

2.4 Implementation Aspects of Geometric Moments

The computation image moments has to be highly accurate to retain the various properties of moment transformations and to have the desired characteristics of moment invariants. In many pattern recognition applications, the speed of computation is also an important factor. The requirement for real-time processing has necessitated hardware implementations of moment based algorithms. This section describes the errors involved in moment computations and also outlines some hardware implementations of image moments.

2.4.1 *Computational Errors*

The following are the major sources of errors in the numerical evaluation of image moments defined in Eq. (2.1):

(1). Image sampling error: The moment definition assumes a continuous coordinate space (x,y). In practice, the image coordinate space is sampled at (or digitized into) discrete points on the image plane, typically from 1 to 512 pixels.

(2). Image quantization error: The moment definition also assumes a continuous intensity function $f(x,y)$. The image data, however consists of quantized gray-level values of the intensity measurements, typically from 1 to 255 gray levels.

(3). Numerical errors: The numerical approximations used to evaluate the moment integrals as well as the round-off errors introduced by the computer word limitations also lead to deviations from the theoretically expected values of the image moments.

(4). Image noise: The noise generated by the optics and the associated electronics can get amplified in the moment computation, and greatly affect the fundamental characteristics of moments and their invariant functions.

A detailed analysis of the noise sensitivity and information redundancy of geometric moments is given in [199]. Here, an auto-correlation function for the intensity function $f(x,y)$ is defined of the form

$$K_{ff}(x,y,u,v) = K_{ff}(0,0)\, e^{-c|x-u|-d|y-v|} \tag{2.85}$$

where c, d are constants and $K_{ff}(0,0) = E\{f(x,y)^2\}$ is the average 'energy' of the image. A white noise process $w(x,y)$ is assumed with zero mean and two-dimensional spectral density σ^2. If w_{pq} denotes the geometric moments of the noise process, then the signal-to-noise ratio of order $p+q$ is

$$SNR_{pq} = \frac{\text{var}\,(m_{pq})}{\text{var}\,(w_{pq})} = \frac{(2p+1)(2q+1)}{4\,\sigma^2} \iiiint (xu)^p\,(yv)^q\,K_{ff}(x,y,u,v)\,dx\,dy\,du\,dv \tag{2.86}$$

A characterization of the digitization and quantization errors in moment calculation in terms of the sampling functions is given in [198].

2.4.2 *Hardware Implementations*

A method to compute the two-dimensional moments using recursive digital filters is given in [24],[34]. The two dimensional moments can be decomposed into two cascaded one-dimensional moments as

$$m_{pq} = \sum_{i=1}^{N} i^p \left\{ \sum_{j=1}^{M} j^q f_{ij} \right\} \tag{2.87}$$

where i, j denote the row and column indices respectively, and f is the intensity value at the pixel (i, j). Here M denotes the total number of rows in the image, and N the total number of columns. The implementation of this algorithm is based on the fact that if the sequence f_n, $n=0,1,2...N$ is applied to the input of a digital filter with impulse response $h(n) = n^k\,u(n)$, where $u(.)$ denotes the step function, then by convolution theorem, the output is

$$y(n) = \sum_{i=1}^{N} h(n-i) \, f_i$$

$$= \sum_{i=1}^{N} (n-i)^k \, f_i \tag{2.88}$$

If the output is evaluated at $n=N$, then we will have

$$y(n) = \sum_{i=1}^{N} (N-i)^k \, f_i \tag{2.89}$$

which is the kth order moment of f_i about the point $n=N$.

The filter implementation for $k=0$ has the transfer function $1/(z-1)$ in the z-transform domain, and is realized with just one adder with one sample delay and a feedback. For the kth order moment, the filter has the transfer function $1/(z-1)^{k+1}$, and is implemented by cascading $k+1$ first-order stages. The detailed implementation aspects are given in [24].

Parallel algorithms suitable for VLSI implementations are discussed in [34]. A similar method for the development of a VLSI based moment generating chip is given in [4].

An optical system to compute the moments of an input image was first proposed by Casasent [26]. Fig. 2.4 shows the schematic diagram of the optical moment computation system. The input image is placed in the input plane P_1, and a moment generating mask is placed in the plane P_2. The mask contains all of the necessary monomials $x^p y^q$ encoded on spatial carriers. When the system is illuminated with coherent light, the pattern in the output plane P_3 contains all the desired moments at distinct locations in the output plane.

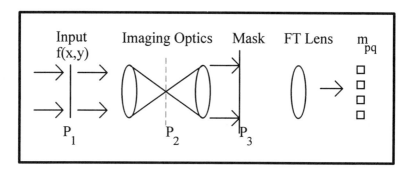

Fig. 2.4 Schematic of optical computation of moments.

Methods for optical computation of moments using the Fourier transforming property of a converging lens were given by Teague [197], and Vijayakumar [207]. Given the Fourier transform $F(u,v)$ of the image plane irradiance distribution f(x, y), the moments m_{pq} can be computed as

$$\left[\frac{\partial^p \partial^q F(u,v)}{\partial u^p \partial v^q}\right]_{u=v=0} = (-2\pi i)^{p+q} \, m_{pq} . \tag{2.90}$$

Optical calculation of moments with this method requires a lens, a phase plate, a network of mirrors, beam splitters and detectors to determine the Fourier transform. The partial derivatives are then estimated by the method of finite differences and measured using strategic spacing of detectors in the Fourier plane.

Casasent [25],[29] has described a hybrid optical/digital processor to optically compute all the moments in parallel.

2.5 Particular Types of Geometric Moments

Two important types of geometric moments are considered in this section. The extension of two-dimensional moments to three dimensions finds applications in the analysis of medical images and range images. Local moments defined over small windows centered around each pixel are used to derive local features for applications in edge detection and texture segmentation.

2.5.1   *Three-dimensional Geometric Moments*

The geometric moments hitherto described in this chapter were defined on a two dimensional image coordinate space (x, y). This definition can be generalised to an n-dimensional space (x_1 , x_2 , ... x_n) as follows:

$$m_{p_1,p_2,\dots p_n} = \int_{x_1 x_2} \int \dots \int_{x_n} x^{p_1} x^{p_2} \dots x^{p_n} \, f(x_1 , x_2 , \dots x_n) \, dx_1 dx_2 \dots dx_n \qquad (2.91)$$

where $p_1,\dots p_n$ are non-negative integers, and 'f' is the n-dimensional density function. The order of the above moment is $p_1 + p_2 + \dots + p_n$. We consider below the three-dimensional geometric moments and their properties.

Three-dimensional geometric moments are the immediate extension of the two-dimensional moments, and have applications in areas where three-dimensional coordinate information is available. For example, when we consider sensor data fusion where the image data obtained from a CCD camera is combined with the range data measured using laser range devices, the three-dimensional moments can be used to characterize the object features. Another application area is medical imaging, where 3D-CAT images can be processed using three-dimensional moments. A pair of stereo images also provide the additional information of depth through binocular parallax, which can be utilized for the computation of three-dimensional moments.

The three-dimensional geometric moments of order $p+q+r$ of a density function $f(x, y, z)$ are given by

$$m_{pqr} = \iiint_{\zeta} x^p y^q z^r \, f(x, y, z) \, dx \, dy \, dz , \qquad\qquad p, q, r = 0,1,2,3\dots \qquad (2.92)$$

Analogous to Eq. (2.7), we can define the moment generating function as

$$M(u, v, w) = \sum_{k=0}^{\infty} \frac{1}{k!} \sum_{p,q,r=0}^{k} \frac{k!}{p!q!r!} m_{pqr} \, u^p \, v^q \, w^r. \qquad (2.93)$$

The coordinates of the centroid can be computed from the first-order moments as follows:

$$x_0 = m_{100} / m_{000} ; \qquad y_0 = m_{010} / m_{000} ; \qquad z_0 = m_{001} / m_{000}. \qquad (2.94)$$

The three-dimensional central moments about the centroid points are denoted by μ_{pqr}. Scale invariance with respect to a uniform scale factor about all the three axes can be achieved by the following normalization scheme:

$$\eta_{pqr} = \mu_{pqr} / (\mu_{000})^{(p+q+r+3)/3} \quad . \tag{2.95}$$

Three-dimensional rotational invariants are obtained using the theory of algebraic invariants, by methods similar to those used in deriving two-dimensional invariants [172]. Two second order invariants are given below as examples.

$$\varphi_1 = \mu_{200} + \mu_{020} + \mu_{002} ,$$

$$\varphi_2 = \mu_{020}\,\mu_{002} - \mu_{011}^{2} + \mu_{200}\,\mu_{002} - \mu_{101}^{2} + \mu_{200}\,\mu_{020} - \mu_{110}^{2}. \tag{2.96}$$

2.5.2 Local Geometric Moments

Local geometric moments are the usual Cartesian moments computed over a small window around each pixel. Local moments are thus associated with image features in a pixel neighborhood, and are used for edge detection [86] and texture segmentation [202].

Consider a window W of size $(2N+1) \times (2N+1)$, with the pixel (x, y) at its center. The $(p+q)^{th}$ order local moment at (x, y) on W is defined as [110]

$$w_{pq}\,(x, y) = \sum_{i=-N}^{N} \sum_{j=-N}^{N} i^p \, j^q \, f(x+i, y+j) \tag{2.97}$$

The above equation gives the discrete computation of local moments, which when viewed as a neighborhood operation, can be interpreted as a convolution of the image with a mask. The masks corresponding to a window size of 3, for the computation of local moments up to order two are given below.

$$w_{00} = \begin{bmatrix} 1 & 1 & 1 \\ 1 & 1 & 1 \\ 1 & 1 & 1 \end{bmatrix}; \qquad w_{10} = \begin{bmatrix} -1 & 0 & 1 \\ -1 & 0 & 1 \\ -1 & 0 & 1 \end{bmatrix}; \qquad w_{01} = \begin{bmatrix} -1 & -1 & -1 \\ 0 & 0 & 0 \\ 1 & 1 & 1 \end{bmatrix};$$

$$w_{11} = \begin{bmatrix} 1 & 0 & -1 \\ 0 & 0 & 0 \\ -1 & 0 & 1 \end{bmatrix}; \quad w_{20} = \begin{bmatrix} 1 & 0 & 1 \\ 1 & 0 & 1 \\ 1 & 0 & 1 \end{bmatrix}; \quad w_{02} = \begin{bmatrix} 1 & 1 & 1 \\ 0 & 0 & 0 \\ 1 & 1 & 1 \end{bmatrix}$$

(2.98)

2.6 Conclusions

The fundamental and theoretical aspects related to geometric moments have been introduced in this chapter. Geometric moments are computationally simple and most widely used in image analysis applications. The characteristics of moments and their shape representation capabilities are briefly outlined. Analytical derivations of different types of invariant functions have been presented. The derivation of rotation invariants based on the theory of algebraic invariants, is given in detail.

The computational aspects of geometric moments are outlined. A few hardware implementations are briefly discussed. Several numerical methods for reducing the computation time and improving the accuracy in the evaluation of moments of thresholded binary images have been described. Two particular types of geometric moments, viz., three-dimensional moments and local moments, have also been discussed.

References

- **Definitions and Properties**: [3], [9], [18], [28], [38], [40], [46], [49], [53], [71], [76], [78], [83], [92], [93], [95], [106], [115], [120], [131], [154], [155], [156], [161], [164], [167], [169], [175], [178], [179], [187], [189], [190], [195], [196], [203], [205], [208], [214], [215], [226].

- **Geometric Moment Invariants**: [7], [11], [12], [14], [21], [33], [39], [51], [56], [57], [58], [59], [60], [62], [69], [75], [77], [85], [88], [89], [90], [117], [120], [128], [143], [155], [166], [168], [195], [211], [212], [213], [218], [219], [220].

- **Fast Computation of Geometric Moments**: [34], [45], [94], [108], [111], [112], [116], [136], [144], [149], [173], [183], [185], [191], [221], [222], [224].

- **Implementation Aspects of Geometric Moments**: [4], [24], [25], [26], [29], [31], [32], [60], [79], [91], [110], [113], [155], [156], [158], [162], [163], [184], [186], [197], [198], [207].

- **Particular Types of Geometric Moments**: [63], [80], [105], [109], [110], [114], [123], [124], [129], [155], [164], [172], [174], [193].

Chapter 3
Complex Moments

The term 'complex moments' is used to encompass all classes of moment functions which have complex kernels. Commonly used functions of this type are radial moments, Fourier-Mellin descriptors and Zernike moments. In addition, a generalization of geometric moments defined in the complex plane is also specifically referred in literature as complex moments. This chapter deals with the above class of moments except Zernike moments. A detailed discussion on Zernike moments is given separately in Chapter 5.

An image transformation of rotation induces a change in the phase angle of complex moments, and therefore the magnitudes of complex moments are rotation invariants. In general, rotation and scale invariants can be easily constructed using complex moments. Invariants of geometrical moments can also be derived in the framework of a moment space with complex basis functions.

3.1 Radial Moments

Radial moments are defined using the polar coordinate representation of the image space, and can be thought of as a more general definition of geometric moments presented in the previous chapter. The main advantage with radial moments is that the image rotations can be directly translated into the corresponding moment transforms, and the expressions for rotation invariants can be easily derived.

The most general definition of a radial moment of order k can be given as follows:

$$\Psi(k, p, q, l) = \int_{r=0}^{\infty} \int_{\theta=0}^{2\pi} r^k \cos^p\theta \, \sin^q\theta \, e^{il\theta} \, g(r, \theta) \, dr \, d\theta \qquad (3.1)$$

where (r, θ) is the image pixel coordinate representation in polar form, and $g(r, \theta)$ is the image intensity distribution. The exponent terms k, p, q, l are integers, and p, q are non-negative. From the above definition, we find that the geometrical moments m_{pq} can be obtained as the following particular case, with the substitutions $x=r\cos\theta$, $y=r\sin\theta$, $dx\,dy = r\,dr\,d\theta$:

$$m_{pq} = \Psi(p+q+1, p, q, 0). \qquad (3.2)$$

We consider below radial moments of the type $\mathcal{Y}(k, 0, 0, l)$ and denote them by $\mathcal{Y}_{kl}$, i.e.,

$$\mathcal{Y}_{kl} = \int\limits_{r=0}^{\infty} \int\limits_{\theta=0}^{2\pi} r^k \, e^{il\theta} \, g(r, \theta) \, dr \, d\theta, \qquad\qquad (i = \sqrt{-1}). \tag{3.3}$$

$\mathcal{Y}_{kl}$ will be referred to as the radial moment of order k with repetition l. The above type of moments were first introduced by Reddi [160].

We now consider the transformation of the radial moments when an image is rotated and scaled. A rotation of the image about the origin by an angle α, and a uniform scale-factor s, induces the following transformation in the polar coordinates:

$$r' = s \, r ; \qquad \theta' = \theta + \alpha . \tag{3.4}$$

The transformed image moments $\mathcal{Y}'_{kl}$ are given by

$$\mathcal{Y}'_{kl} = s^{k+1} \, e^{il\alpha} \, \mathcal{Y}_{kl} . \tag{3.5}$$

From the above expression, we can easily construct functions of $\mathcal{Y}_{kl}$ which are invariant with respect to the scale-factor s, and the rotation angle α.

3.1.1 *Rotation and Scale Invariants*

Eq. (3.5) gives an important property of radial moments, that an image rotation (by an angle α), and scale variation (by a factor s) directly correspond to a transformation of the moment vector in the complex plane by a rotation (through an angle $l\alpha$), and a scale change (by a factor s^{k+1}).

From Eq. (3.5) we get

$$\mathcal{Y}'_{00} = s \, \mathcal{Y}_{00}. \tag{3.6}$$

Eliminating s from Eqs. (3.5) and (3.6) we have

$$\mathcal{Y}'_{kl} / (\mathcal{Y}'_{00})^{k+1} = \mathcal{Y}_{kl} / (\mathcal{Y}_{00})^{k+1}, \tag{3.7}$$

which shows that the term $\mathcal{Y}_{kl} / (\mathcal{Y}_{00})^{k+1}$ is scale invariant.

Again from Eq. (3.5) we find that the terms Ψ_{k0}, $|\Psi_{kl}|^2$ are rotation invariant. In general, an expression of the form $\Psi_{kl}(\Psi_{pl})^*$ is an invariant under rotation. Thus, a set of functions of radial moments which are invariant with respect to both rotation and scale variation, can be formed as given below.

$$\vartheta_1 = \Psi_{k0} / (\Psi_{00})^{k+1},$$

$$\vartheta_2 = |\Psi_{kl}|^2 / (\Psi_{00})^{2(k+1)},$$

$$\vartheta_3 = \Psi_{kl}(\Psi_{pl})^* / (\Psi_{00})^{k+p+2}. \tag{3.8}$$

The above functions, however, are not invariant with respect to image translation. Image translation cannot be directly represented as a linear transformation of the polar coordinates. Translation invariance can be indirectly achieved by first computing the image centroid point using geometric moments [Eq. (2.9)] and then shifting the origin of the polar coordinate system to the centroid point.

3.1.2 *Derivation of Geometric Moment Invariants*

Here we use the rotational invariants derived in the previous section to obtain the invariant polynomials of geometric moments. The radial moments of the type $\Psi_{2k+l+1, l}$ can be expressed in the form

$$\Psi_{2k+l+1, l} = \iint_{x\,y} (x^2+y^2)^k (x+iy)^l \ f(x, y) \ dx \ dy . \tag{3.9}$$

The integral term in the above equation can be expanded using binomial theorem to get a complex polynomial of geometric moments. Rotational invariants of geometric moments can now be generated using expressions of the type Ψ_{k0}, $|\Psi_{kl}|^2$ in Eq. (3.9). For example,

$$\Psi_{30} = m_{20} + m_{02} ,$$

$$|\Psi_{31}|^2 = (m_{30} + m_{12})^2 + (m_{21} + m_{03})^2 ,$$

$$|\Psi_{32}|^2 = (m_{20} - m_{02})^2 + 4m_{11}^2,$$

$$|\Psi_{03}|^2 = (m_{30} - 3m_{12})^2 + (3m_{21} - m_{03})^2. \tag{3.10}$$

The above set of rotational invariants of geometric moments were earlier obtained using a more complicated procedure based on the theory of algebraic invariants [see section (2.2.4) and Eq. (2.34)]. The transformation given in Eq.(3.5) is particularly suitable for deriving the invariant functions.

3.2 Fourier-Mellin Descriptors

Fourier-Mellin descriptors (also referred to as Fourier-Mellin moments) of order k and repetition l are defined as

$$F_{kl} = \int_{r=0}^{\infty} \int_{\theta=0}^{2\pi} r^{k-1} e^{-il\theta} g(r, \theta) \, dr \, d\theta. \qquad (i = \sqrt{-1}) \qquad (3.11)$$

The integral in the above equation is another form of radial moments, which combines the radial Mellin transform

$$M_k = \int_{r=0}^{\infty} r^{k-1} g(r) \, dr, \qquad (3.12)$$

and the circular-harmonic Fourier transform

$$F_l = \frac{1}{2\pi} \int_{\theta=0}^{2\pi} e^{-il\theta} g(\theta) \, d\theta. \qquad (3.13)$$

From the definition given in Eq. (3.3) we get

$$F_{kl} = \Psi_{k-1,\,-l}. \qquad (3.14)$$

3.2.1 Fourier-Mellin Invariants

The radial-Mellin part of the moments is used to achieve scale invariance, and the circular-harmonic expansion is used to achieve rotation invariance. A scale transformation $r' = s\, r$ induces the following transformation in F_{kl}:

$$F'_{kl} = s^k F_{kl}. \qquad (3.15)$$

Thus, the expressions $\dfrac{F_{kl}}{(F_{20})^{k/2}}$ and $\dfrac{(F_{kl})^2}{(F_{k0})^2}$ are scale invariant.

Similarly, the terms F_{k0}, $|F_{kl}|^2$ are rotation invariant.

It is also easy to see that the geometric moment invariants given in Eq. (3.10) correspond to the functions F_{40}, $|F_{51}|^2$, $|F_{42}|^2$, $|F_{53}|^2$ respectively.

3.2.2 *Orthogonal Fourier-Mellin Descriptors*

The kernel of the Fourier-Mellin transform defined in Eq. (3.11) is not orthogonal. Orthogonal functions additionally yield independent descriptors of the image shape, thereby increasing the information content, and minimizing information redundancy among a set of moments. The orthogonalization of Fourier-Mellin descriptors is described in [182]. Consider the following generalization of the Eq. (3.11), with the domain of the function 'g' restricted to the interior of a unit circle:

$$\Phi_{pq} = \frac{1}{2\pi a_p} \int_{r=0}^{1} \int_{\theta=0}^{2\pi} Q_p(r)\, e^{-iq\theta}\, g(r,\theta)\, r\, dr\, d\theta, \qquad (3.16)$$

where $Q_p(r)$ is a polynomial in r of degree n, and a_p is a normalization constant. We now impose the condition that the functions $Q_p(r)$ are orthogonal inside the unit circle, i.e.,

$$\int_{r=0}^{1} Q_p(r)\, Q_k(r)\, r dr = a_p\, \delta_{pk} \qquad (3.17)$$

where δ_{pk} is the Kronecker symbol.

We obtain the polynomials $Q_p(r)$ by applying Gram-Schmidt orthogonalization process to the sequence of natural powers of r as given below [182].

$$Q_p(r) = \sum_{s=0}^{p} \alpha_{ps}\, r^s, \qquad (3.18)$$

where

$$\alpha_{ps} = (-1)^{p+s} \frac{(p+s+1)!}{(p-s)!\, s!\, (s+1)!} \,, \tag{3.19}$$

and the normalization constant is given by

$$a_p = \frac{1}{2(p+1)} \tag{3.20}$$

The Fourier-Mellin descriptors F_{kl} given in Eq. (3.11) can be related to the orthogonal functions Φ_{pq} of Eq. (3.16), as follows:

$$\Phi_{pq} = \frac{(p+1)}{\pi} \sum_{k=0}^{p} \alpha_{pk} F_{k-2,\,q} \,. \tag{3.21}$$

3.2.3 *Inverse Orthogonal Fourier-Mellin Transform*

The kernel of the Fourier-Mellin moments Φ_{pq} as given in Eq. (3.16) form a complete orthogonal basis set. The image intensity function can therefore be reconstructed using the Fourier expansion theorem on orthogonal functions. The following equation is called the inverse Fourier-Mellin transform:

$$f(r,\theta) = \sum_p \sum_q \Phi_{pq}\, Q_p(r)\, e^{iq\theta}. \tag{3.22}$$

Using only a finite set of moments Φ_{pq} , $-M \le q \le M$, $0 \le p \le N$, where M, N are positive integers; an approximate version $f'(r,\theta)$ of the intensity function can be reconstructed as

$$f'(r,\theta) = \sum_{p=0}^{N} \sum_{q=-M}^{M} \Phi_{pq}\, Q_p(r)\, e^{iq\theta}. \tag{3.23}$$

Theoretically, moment functions with an orthogonal set as kernel, can represent independent characteristics of the image shape, without any information redundancy. A finite set of moments can thus represent in sufficient detail the image shape, since the image can be approximately reconstructed from those moments.

3.2.4 *Noise Sensitivity of Orthogonal Fourier-Mellin Moments*

Assuming that the image is corrupted by a zero-mean additive white noise with the auto-correlation function $K_{ff}(r,\theta,\rho,\phi)$ as defined in Section 2.4.1, and represented in the polar form, the statistical signal-to-noise ratio of the orthogonal Fourier-Mellin descriptors can be defined as [182],[199]

$$SNR_{pq} = \frac{\text{var}\,(\Phi_{pq})}{\text{var}\,(w_{pq})} = \frac{1}{\sigma^2} \int_0^{2\pi} \int_0^1 \int_0^{2\pi} \int_0^1 Q_p(r)\, Q_p(\rho)\, K_{ff}(r,\theta,\rho,\phi)\, \cos[q(\theta-\phi)]\; r\,dr\,d\theta\; \rho\,d\rho\, d\phi$$

$$(3.24)$$

where w_{pq} are the orthogonal Fourier-Mellin moments of the noise process.

3.3 Moment Definitions in the Complex Plane

The image coordinate space can be considered as a complex plane, with the pixel coordinates represented by complex numbers $z = x + iy$ $(i=\sqrt{-1})$. The geometric moments defined in the previous chapter can be generalized to the following moments in the complex plane.

The $(p+q)^{\text{th}}$ order complex moments C_{pq} about a point c are given by

$$C_{pq} = \int_{z\in\zeta} (z-c)^p\, (z-c)^{*q}\, f(z)\, dz, \qquad p, q = 0,1,2,3.... \qquad (3.25)$$

where z, c are complex numbers representing points on the image plane ζ, and $*$ denotes complex conjugate. Eq. (3.25) can be written in terms of the Cartesian image coordinates (x, y) to obtain the moment expressions about the origin $(c=0)$ as

$$C_{pq} = \iint_{\zeta} (x+iy)^p\, (x-iy)^q\, f(x, y)\, dx\, dy. \qquad p, q = 0,1,2,3....$$

$$(3.26)$$

The above moment has also the following representation in polar form

$$C_{pq} = \int_{r=0}^{\infty} \int_{\theta=0}^{2\pi} r^{p+q+1}\, e^{i(p-q)\theta}\, g(r, \theta)\, dr\, d\theta, \qquad (3.27)$$

and hence it is related to the radial moments [Eq. (3.1)] as

$$C_{pq} = \Psi(p+q+1, 0, 0, p-q). \tag{3.28}$$

Eq. (3.26) can be used to relate complex moments and geometric moments. For example,

$$C_{00} = m_{00} \, ,$$

$$C_{10} = m_{10} + i \, m_{01} \, ,$$

$$C_{11} = m_{20} + m_{02} \, ,$$

$$C_{20} = m_{20} - m_{02} + 2 \, i \, m_{11} \, . \tag{3.29}$$

From Eqs. (2.14),(2.15), we find that the image ellipse parameters I_1 , I_2, θ can be conveniently expressed in complex moments as

$$I_1 = (C_{11} + | \, C_{20}| \,) \, /2 \, ,$$

$$I_2 = (C_{11} - | \, C_{20}| \,) \, /2 \, ,$$

$$\theta = \mathrm{Arg}(C_{20}) \, /2. \tag{3.30}$$

We also note that

$$C_{pq} = C_{qp}^{*} \, ,$$

$$C_{pp} = m_{2p,0} + m_{0,2p} \, . \tag{3.31}$$

Rotation and scale invariant expressions in C_{pq} can be derived using methods similar to those given in Section 3.1.1. The transformed moments C_{pq}' corresponding to an image rotation by an angle α can be got as

$$C_{pq}' = C_{pq} \, e^{i(p-q)\alpha} \, , \tag{3.32}$$

and therefore the terms $|C_{pq}|$ are rotation invariant.

In general, the term, $C_{rs} \, C_{tu}^{k} + C_{sr} \, C_{ut}^{k}$ is rotation invariant if

$$(r-s) + k \, (t-u) = 0. \tag{3.33}$$

The above condition eliminates the imaginary part and the rotational phase factor from the moment expression, yielding real-valued rotational invariants. It is also easy to see that the term $C_{pq}/(C_{00})^{(p+q+2)/2}$ is scale invariant.

The complex moments C_{pq} are related to the orthogonal Fourier-Mellin moments Φ_{pq} by the following equation: [182]

$$\Phi_{pq} = \frac{(p+1)}{\pi} \sum_{s=0}^{p} \alpha_{ps} \, C_{(s-q)/2, \, (s+q)/2}, \qquad (3.34)$$

where the coefficients α_{ps} are given in Eq. (3.19).

3.4 Implementation Aspects of Complex Moments

The basis functions of the complex moments are usually defined in polar coordinates (r, θ), which further necessitates the image intensity function to be defined accordingly. Since the most common type of image data representation is in Cartesian coordinates, the conversion to a polar reference system imposes additional overhead in complex moment computations. In general, complex moments are much more difficult to implement than geometric moments, but provides a suitable framework for the development of analytical results such as general expressions for invariants. A method for evaluating the complex moments of a binary image is discussed below.

If a binary image is represented by a set of its boundary points in polar coordinates $\{r_\theta : \ 0 \le \theta \le 2\pi\}$, where r_θ denotes the radial distance to the boundary point situated at an angle θ, then the complex moment Ψ_{kl} in Eq. (3.3) can be evaluated as

$$\Psi_{kl} = \int_0^{2\pi} \left\{ \int_0^{r_\theta} r^k \, dr \right\} e^{il\theta} \, d\theta. \qquad (3.35)$$

The above expression can be further reduced to the following discrete form:

$$\Psi_{kl} = \left(\frac{1}{k+1} \right) \sum_{\theta=0}^{2\pi} \left\{ r_\theta^{k+1} (\cos l\theta + i \sin l\theta) \right\} \Delta\theta, \qquad (3.36)$$

where $\Delta\theta$ is the incremental angle between successive boundary points.

3.5 Conclusions

The generalization of geometric moments with complex kernel functions has been considered in this chapter. A convenient representation of complex kernels is using a polar form of the image coordinate space, and this helps in easily deriving the rotation and scale invariants. Invariants of geometric moments can also be derived from complex moments, without using the theory of algebraic invariants. The relevant mathematical details of the radial, Fourier-Mellin, and complex-domain moments have been presented. An orthogonal version of Fourier-Mellin functions is also introduced in this chapter.

References

• **Radial Moments**: [47], [155], [160], [199].

• **Fourier-Mellin Descriptors**: [5], [6], [64], [72], [74], [87], [117], [118], [180], [181], [182], [219].

• **Moment Definitions in the Complex Plane**: [1], [2], [17], [39], [60], [125], [126], [133], [147], [155], [199].

• **Implementation Aspects of Complex Moments**: [1],[141].

Chapter 4
Legendre Moments

Moments with an orthogonal basis can be used to attain a zero value of redundancy measure in a set of moment functions, so that the moments correspond to independent characteristics of the image. The image intensity distribution can also be analytically reconstructed from its orthogonal moments. The Legendre polynomials form a complete orthogonal set inside the unit circle. Moments with the Legendre polynomials as kernel functions were first introduced by Teague [196].

4.1 Definitions and Properties

The kernel of Legendre moments are products of Legendre polynomials defined along rectangular image coordinate axes inside a unit circle. The Legendre moments of order $(p+q)$ are defined as

$$L_{pq} = \frac{(2p+1)(2q+1)}{4} \int_{-1}^{1} \int_{-1}^{1} P_p(x)\, P_q(y)\, f(x,y)\, dx\, dy \qquad (4.1)$$

where the functions $P_n(x)$ denote Legendre polynomial of order n [Section 4.1.1]. The Legendre moments L_{pq} generalizes the geometric moments m_{pq} [Eq. (2.1)] in the sense that the monomial $x^p y^q$ is replaced by the orthogonal polynomial $P_p(x)\, P_q(y)$ of the same order.

In order to evaluate the Legendre moments, the image coordinate space has to be necessarily scaled so that their respective magnitudes are less than 1. If the image dimension along each coordinate axis is N pixels, and i, j denote the pixel coordinate indices along the axes, then $0 \le i, j \le N$, and the discrete version of the Legendre moments can be written as

$$L_{pq} = \frac{(2p+1)(2q+1)}{(N-1)^2} \sum_{i=1}^{N} \sum_{j=1}^{N} P_p(x_i)\, P_q(y_j)\, f(i,j) \qquad (4.2)$$

where x_i, y_j denote the normalized pixel coordinates in the range $[-1, 1]$, given by

$$x_i = (2\,i\,/\,N) - 1\,; \qquad y_j = (2\,j\,/\,N) - 1. \qquad (4.3)$$

49

4.1.1 *Legendre Polynomials*

We summarize below some important definitions and properties related to Legendre polynomials which will be useful in our subsequent discussion on Legendre moments. The Legendre polynomial $P_n(x)$ of order n is defined as

$$P_n(x) = \sum_{k=0}^{n} (-1)^{(n-k)/2} \frac{1}{2^n} \frac{(n+k)!\; x^k}{\left(\dfrac{n-k}{2}\right)! \left(\dfrac{n+k}{2}\right)!\, k!}, \qquad |x| \le 1, \text{ and } (n-k) \text{ is even.}$$

(4.4)

The above series expansion of Legendre polynomials can be obtained from the equation

$$P_n(x) = \frac{1}{2^n\, n!} \frac{d^n (x^2-1)^n}{d x^n}$$

(4.5)

The Legendre polynomials form a complete orthogonal set inside the unit circle, and hence

$$\int_{-1}^{1} P_m(x)\, P_n(x)\; dx = \frac{2}{2m+1}\, \delta_{mn}$$

(4.6)

The following equation provides a recursive relation in Legendre polynomials:

$$P_n(x) = \frac{(2n-1)\, x\, P_{n-1}(x) - (n-1)\, P_{n-2}(x)}{n},$$

(4.7)

where

$$P_0(x) = 1; \qquad P_1(x) = x; \qquad |x| \le 1; \qquad \text{and,} \qquad n > 1.$$

The integral formula for Legendre polynomials is given by

$$\int P_n(x)\, dx = \frac{x\, P_n(x) - P_{n-1}(x)}{n+1}.$$

(4.8)

The plots of the functions $P_n(x)$, $n=1..6$, are given in Fig. 4.1.

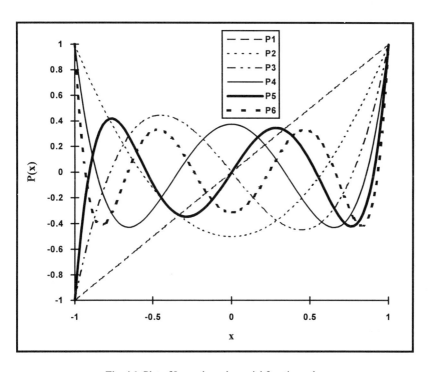

Fig. 4.1 Plot of Legendre polynomial function values.

The polynomial expressions for $P_n(x)$ up to the fourth order are given below.

$$P_0(x) = 1$$

$$P_1(x) = x$$

$$P_2(x) = (3x^2-1)/2$$

$$P_3(x) = (5x^3-3x)/2$$

$$P_4(x) = (35x^4-30x^2+3)/8 .$$ (4.9)

4.1.2 *Equations Relating Legendre and Geometric Moments*

The Legendre moments of order $(p+q)$ can be expressed in terms of geometric moments as follows [196],[199]:

$$L_{pq} = \frac{(2p+1)(2q+1)}{4} \sum_{i=0}^{p} \sum_{j=0}^{q} a_{pi} a_{qj} m_{ij}, \tag{4.10}$$

where a_{pi} denotes the coefficient of x^i in the series expansion of $P_p(x)$ as given in Eq. (4.4). From the above equation, we find that the Legendre moments depend at most on the geometric moments of the same order or lower, and conversely. Assigning particular values for p, q in Eq. (4.10), we get the following relations in Legendre moments up to the second order.

$L_{00} = m_{00}$,

$L_{10} = (3/4) \, m_{10}$,

$L_{01} = (3/4) \, m_{01}$,

$L_{20} = (5/4) \, [\, (3/2) \, m_{20} - (1/2) \, m_{00} \,]$,

$L_{02} = (5/4) \, [\, (3/2) \, m_{02} - (1/2) \, m_{00} \,]$,

$L_{11} = (9/4) \, m_{11}$,

$L_{30} = (7/4) \, [\, (5/2) \, m_{30} - (3/2) \, m_{10} \,]$,

$L_{03} = (7/4) \, [\, (5/2) \, m_{03} - (3/2) \, m_{01} \,]$,

$L_{21} = (15/4) \, [\, (3/2) \, m_{21} - (1/2) \, m_{01} \,]$,

$L_{12} = (15/4) \, [\, (3/2) \, m_{12} - (1/2) \, m_{10} \,]$. $\hspace{2cm}$ (4.11)

Since Legendre moments are defined only inside the unit circle, the above equations are valid only if the geometric moments are evaluated after scaling the pixel coordinates to the range $[-1, 1]$, using Eq. (4.3).

4.1.3 *Inverse Legendre Moment Transform*

The orthogonality property of the Legendre polynomials helps in expressing the image intensity function $f(x,y)$ in terms of its Legendre moments using the Fourier expansion theorem on orthogonal functions. The following equation is called the inverse Legendre moment transform:

$$f(x,y) = \sum_{i=0}^{\infty} \sum_{j=0}^{\infty} L_{ij}\, P_i(x)\, P_j(y), \qquad |x|, |y| \le 1. \tag{4.12}$$

From a finite number n of Legendre moments, an approximate version $f'(x,y)$ of the intensity function can be reconstructed as follows [196]:

$$f'(x,y) = \sum_{i=0}^{n} \sum_{j=0}^{i} L_{i-j,j}\, P_{i-j}(x)\, P_j(y), \qquad |x|, |y| \le 1. \tag{4.13}$$

An example of image reconstruction using Legendre moments, is given later in Chapter 9.

4.1.4 *Noise Sensitivity of Legendre Moments*

Assuming an auto-correlation function $K_{ff}(x,y,u,v)$ for the intensity function $f(x,y)$ defined as in Eq. (2.86), and an image corrupted by a white noise process $w(x,y)$ with zero mean and two-dimensional spectral density σ^2, we can define the signal-to-noise ratio as follows [199]:

$$SNR_{pq} = \frac{\text{var }(L_{pq})}{\text{var }(w_{pq})} = \frac{(2p+1)(2q+1)}{4\,\sigma^2} \iiiint P_m(x)\, P_m(u)\, P_n(y)\, P_n(v)\, K_{ff}(x,y,u,v)\, dx\, dy\, du\, dv$$

$$\tag{4.14}$$

where w_{pq} denotes the Legendre moments of the noise process.

4.2 Fast Computation of Legendre Moments

This section describes methods for the fast computation of Legendre moments. The recursive relation and integral formula for Legendre polynomials are made use of in the following algorithms.

4.2.1 *Contour Integration Method for Binary Images*

For a binary image with unit intensity function, the surface integral for evaluating Legendre moments given in Eq. (4.1) can be converted to a contour integral with the help of Green's theorem given in Eq. (2.76), where the scalar point function Q is defined such that

$$\partial Q / \partial x = P_p(x)\, P_q(y) . \tag{4.15}$$

Using the contour integral formula in Eq. (2.76), and Eqs. (4.8), we get the expression for the $(p+q)^{\text{th}}$ order Legendre moment as

$$L_{pq} = \frac{(2p+1)\,(2q+1)}{4\,(p+1)} \int_C \{x\, P_p(x) - P_{p-1}(x)\}\, P_q(y)\, dy \tag{4.16}$$

where 'C' is the edge contour of the image. Representing the image boundary by the end-point coordinates given in Eq. (2.67) as $(<x_{1k},\ x_{2k}>,\ y_k)$, $k=0,1,2,\ldots n$, and denoting

$$T_k = [x\, P_p(x) - P_{p-1}(x)]\,_{x=x_{1k}}^{x=x_{2k}} , \tag{4.17}$$

we can apply mean-value theorem of integrals on each image row to get the following discrete form:

$$L_{pq} = \frac{(2p+1)(2q+1)}{4(p+1)} \sum_{k=1}^{n-1} \frac{(T_k + T_{k+1})}{2} \Delta y \tag{4.18}$$

where

$$T_k = P_q(y_k).[x_{2k}\, P_p(x_{2k}) - P_{p-1}(x_{2k}) - x_{1k}\, P_p(x_{1k}) + P_{p-1}(x_{1k})]. \tag{4.19}$$

If N is the number of pixels along each image axis, then we have

$$\Delta y = 2/(N-1), \tag{4.20}$$

as a result of the scaling of the image coordinates in the range $[1, N]$ to the range $[-1, 1]$.

Substituting for Δy in Eq. (4.18) we get

$$L_{pq} = \frac{(2p+1)(2q+1)}{4(p+1)(N-1)} \sum_{k=1}^{n-1}(T_k + T_{k+1}) \ . \tag{4.21}$$

The above equation involves only the boundary points of the image. We can also use the recursive relation (4.7) in evaluating the Legendre polynomials to further reduce the computation time.

4.2.2 *Computation of Legendre moments of Gray-level Images*

The pseudo-code for fast computation of Legendre moments is given in Fig. 4.2 below [141].

Legend:
    max = Maximum order of Legendre moments to be computed
    N = Image size in pixels
    $P(p, i)$ = Legendre polynomial array (i = row/column index)

Compute and store Legendre polynomial values:
    For i = 1, N
        $x = (2i/N)-1$ (Normalize image coordinates)
        $P(0, i) = 1$
        $P(1, i) = x$
        For p =2 to max (Store polynomial values)
            $P(p, i) = \{(2p-1) \, x \, P(p-1,i) - (p-1) \, P(p-2,i)\} \, / \, p$
        end
    end

Compute Legendre moments of the image:
    For p = 0 to max
        For q = 0 to max
            Sum = $\sum_i \sum_j P(p, i) \, P(q, j) \, f(i, j)$
            L_{pq} = $(2p+1) \, (2q+1)$ Sum $/(N-1)^2$
        end
    end

Fig. 4.2 Pseudo-code for fast computation of Legendre moments.

In the above algorithm, the Legendre moments of gray-level images are computed by applying the recursive formula in Eq. (4.7). The Legendre polynomials up to the required order of moments are evaluated once for a complete row index, and used in the discrete summation formula given in Eq. (4.2).

4.3 Conclusions

Legendre moments and their properties have been introduced in this chapter. The orthogonality property of the Legendre polynomials enables the construction of independent Legendre moments, providing minimum information redundancy among the feature descriptors. The recursive relation and the integral formula of Legendre polynomials have been effectively utilized in reducing the computation time, and to evolve a contour-integration method for obtaining the Legendre moments of binary images. The image intensity distribution can be approximately reconstructed from a set of Legendre moments of the image, using the Fourier expansion theorem.

References

- **Definitions and Properties**: [8], [17], [40], [82], [119], [134], [146], [152], [155], [170], [177], [196], [199], [204].

- **Fast Computation of Legendre Moments**: [141].

Chapter 5
Zernike Moments

Zernike Moments were first introduced by Teague [196] based on the orthogonal functions called Zernike polynomials[225]. Though computationally very complex compared to geometric and Legendre moments, Zernike moments have proved to be superior in terms of their feature representation capability and low noise sensitivity [14],[199].

5.1 Definitions and Properties

The kernel of Zernike moments are orthogonal Zernike polynomials defined over the polar coordinates inside a unit circle. The Zernike moment of order p is defined as

$$Z_{pq} = \frac{(p+1)}{\pi} \int_0^{2\pi} \int_0^1 V_{pq}^*(r,\theta)\, f(r,\theta)\, r\, dr\, d\theta \quad , \qquad r \le 1. \tag{5.1}$$

In the above expression, p is a non-negative integer, and q is an integer such that

$$p-|q| \text{ is even, and, } |q| \le p. \tag{5.2}$$

The functions $V_{pq}(r,\theta)$ denote Zernike polynomials of order p with repetition q, and * denotes complex conjugate. A detailed description of Zernike polynomials is given in Section 5.1.1.

If N is the number of pixels along each axis of the image, then Eq. (5.1) can be written in the discrete form

$$Z_{pq} = \frac{(p+1)}{\pi(N-1)^2} \sum_{x=1}^{N} \sum_{y=1}^{N} V_{pq}^*(r,\theta)\, f(x,y) \tag{5.3}$$

where

$$r = (x^2 + y^2)^{\frac{1}{2}} / N, \text{ and, } \theta = \tan^{-1}(y/x).$$

5.1.1   *Zernike Polynomials*

Zernike polynomials $V_{nm}(r,\theta)$ of order n are defined as functions of the polar coordinates r, θ as

$$V_{nm}(r,\theta) = R_{nm}(r)\, e^{im\theta} \tag{5.4}$$

where $R_{nm}(r)$ is a real-valued radial polynomial given by

$$R_{nm}(r) = \sum_{s=0}^{(n-|m|)/2} (-1)^s \frac{(n-s)!}{s!\left(\dfrac{n-2s+|m|}{2}\right)!\left(\dfrac{n-2s-|m|}{2}\right)!}\, r^{n-2s} \tag{5.5}$$

$$n = 0,1,2,......\infty; \qquad 0 \le |m| \le n; \ \text{and}, \ n-|m| \ \text{is even.}$$

The orthogonality condition on the Zernike polynomials gives

$$\int_0^{2\pi}\int_0^1 V_{nl}^{*}(r,\theta)\, V_{mk}(r,\theta)\, r\, dr\, d\theta = \frac{\pi}{(n+1)}\, \delta_{nm}\, \delta_{lk}, \tag{5.6}$$

where δ_{nm} denotes the Kronecker-delta. The radial polynomials $R_{nm}(r)$ satisfy the relation

$$\int_0^1 R_{nl}(r)\, R_{ml}(r)\, r\, dr = \frac{1}{2(n+1)}\, \delta_{nm}. \tag{5.7}$$

From Eq. (5.4) , we get

$$V_{nm}(r,\theta) = [V_{n,-m}(r,\theta)]^{*}. \tag{5.8}$$

Some important properties of the radial polynomial in Eq. (5.5) are given below.

$$R_{nm}(1) = 1,$$

$$R_{nn}(r) = r^n,$$

$$R_{00}(r) = 1,$$

$$R_{2n,0}(r) = P_n(2r^2-1). \tag{5.9}$$

In the above equation, P_n is the Legendre polynomial of order n. The polynomial expressions for $R_{nm}(r)$ up to the order of 7 are given in Table 5.1 [19].

n \ m	0	1	2	3	4	5	6	7
0	1	-	$2r^2-1$	-	$6r^4-6r^2+1$	-	$20r^6-30r^4+12r^2-1$	-
1	-	r	-	$3r^3-2r$	-	$10r^5-12r^3+3r$	-	$35r^7-60r^5+30r^3-4r$
2	-	-	r^2	-	$4r^4-3r^2$	-	$15r^6-20r^4+6r^2$	-
3	-	-	-	r^3	-	$5r^5-4r^3$	-	$21r^7-30r^5+10r^3$
4	-	-	-	-	r^4	-	$6r^6-5r^4$	-
5	-	-	-	-	-	r^5	-	$7r^7-6r^5$
6	-	-	-	-	-	-	r^6	-
7	-	-	-	-	-	-	-	r^7

Table 5.1 Radial polynomial expressions for $R_{nm}(r)$.

By replacing the index $(n-2s)$ by k in Eq. (5.5), we can rewrite the radial polynomials in powers of r as follows:

$$R_{nm} = \sum_{k=m}^{n} B_{nmk} r^k, \qquad (m \geq 0,\ n-k \text{ is even}) \qquad (5.10)$$

where

$$B_{nmk} = \frac{(-1)^{(n-k)/2} \left(\dfrac{n+k}{2}\right)!}{\left(\dfrac{n-k}{2}\right)! \left(\dfrac{k+m}{2}\right)! \left(\dfrac{k-m}{2}\right)!}. \qquad (5.11)$$

From Eq. (5.10) it is easy to derive the following straight-forward relationship between Zernike moments and radial moments [Eq.(3.3)]:

$$Z_{nm} = \sum_{k=m}^{n} B_{nmk} \psi_{km}, \qquad (n-k \text{ is even}). \qquad (5.12)$$

5.1.2 Pseudo-Zernike Moments

Pseudo-Zernike moments are also defined in terms of orthogonal basis functions inside the unit circle, and the corresponding polynomials have properties analogous to that of Zernike polynomials. The real-valued pseudo-Zernike polynomials $S_{nm}(r)$ are defined as

$$S_{nm}(r) = \sum_{s=0}^{n-|m|} (-1)^s \frac{(2n+1-s)!}{s! \, (n-|m|-s)! \, (n+|m|+1-s)!} \, r^{n-s} \tag{5.13}$$

$$n=0,1,2,....\infty; \quad 0 \le |m| \le n.$$

The moment functions in Eq.(5.1), with the polynomials $S_{nm}(r)$ in place of $R_{nm}(r)$ in Eq.(5.4), are called the pseudo-Zernike moments $\tilde{Z}_{pq}$, i.e.,

$$\tilde{Z}_{pq} = \frac{(p+1)}{\pi} \int_0^{2\pi} \int_0^1 S_{pq}(r) \, e^{-iq\theta} \, f(r,\theta) \, r \, dr \, d\theta \, , \qquad r \le 1. \tag{5.14}$$

Eq.(5.13) can also be expressed as

$$S_{nm}(r) = \sum_{k=m}^{n} C_{nmk} \, r^k$$

where

$$C_{nmk} = \frac{(-1)^{n-k} (n+k+1)!}{(n-k)! \, (k+m+1)! \, (k-m)!}. \tag{5.15}$$

The polynomial expressions for $S_{nm}(r)$ up to the order of 4 are given in Table 5.2 below.

n \ m	0	1	2	3	4
0	1	$3r-2$	$10r^2-12r+3$	$35r^3-60r^2+30r-4$	$126r^4-280r^3+210r^2-60r+5$
1	-	r	$5r^2-4r$	$21r^3-30r^2+10r$	$84r^4-168r^3+105r^2-20r$
2	-	-	r^2	$7r^3-6r^2$	$36r^4-56r^3+21r^2$
3	-	-	-	r^3	$9r^4-8r^3$
4	-	-	-	-	r^4

Table 5.2 Radial polynomial expressions for $S_{nm}(r)$.

The pseudo-Zernike moments can be expressed in terms of radial moments as

$$\tilde{Z}_{nm} = \sum_{k=m}^{n} C_{nmk} \, \psi_{km} \, . \tag{5.16}$$

The set of pseudo-Zernike polynomials of order $\leq n$, contain $(n+1)^2$ linearly independent polynomials of degree $\leq n$. The set of Zernike polynomials contain only $(n+1)$ $(n+2)/2$ linearly independent polynomials of degree $\leq n$, due to the additional condition that $n-|m|$ is even.

5.1.3 *Equations Relating Zernike and Geometric Moments*

Eq. (5.10) provides a convenient way to express Zernike moments in terms of geometric moments. Using this equation in the Zernike moment definition, we get

$$Z_{nm} = \frac{n+1}{\pi} \sum_{k=m}^{n} B_{nmk} \int_{0}^{2\pi} \int_{0}^{1} r^k \, e^{-im\theta} \, f(r,\theta) \, r \, dr \, d\theta, \qquad r \leq 1. \tag{5.17}$$

In Cartesian form, the above equation can be written as

$$Z_{nm} = \frac{n+1}{\pi} \sum_{k=m}^{n} B_{nmk} \int_{x} \int_{y} (x-iy)^m \, (x^2+y^2)^{(k-m)/2} \, f(x,y) \, dx \, dy \, . \tag{5.18}$$

The integral on the right-hand side can now be easily expressed as a series of geometric moment functions. The equations relating Zernike and geometric moments up to the third order are given below.

$Z_{00} = (1/\pi) \, m_{00}$

$Z_{11} = (2/\pi) \, (m_{10} - i \, m_{01})$

$Z_{20} = (6/\pi) \, (m_{20} + m_{02}) - (3/\pi) \, m_{00}$

$Z_{22} = (3/\pi) \, (m_{20} - m_{02} - 2i \, m_{11})$

$Z_{31} = (12/\pi) \, (m_{30} + m_{12}) - (12/\pi)i \, (m_{03} + m_{21}) - (8/\pi) \, (m_{10} - i \, m_{01})$

$Z_{33} = (4/\pi) \, (m_{30} - 3m_{12}) + (4/\pi)i \, (m_{03} - 3m_{21})$ $\hfill (5.19)$

Since the Zernike moments are defined inside the unit circle, the above equations are valid only when the geometric moments are evaluated for the normalized pixel coordinates transformed to the range $[-1,1]$.

Analytical expressions for the Zernike moments of a general ellipse are given in Appendix 2.

5.1.4 *Inverse Zernike Moment Transform*

The image intensity function $f(x, y)$ can be reconstructed from a finite number n of Zernike moments, using the Fourier expansion theorem on orthogonal functions, as

$$f(r,\theta) \cong \sum_{p=0}^{n} \sum_{q} Z_{pq} V_{pq}(r,\theta), \qquad |q| \le p, \ p-|q| \text{ is even.} \tag{5.20}$$

The Zernike moment Z_{pq} and the Zernike polynomials $V_{pq}(r,\theta)$ are complex-valued, but the image intensity function $f(r,\theta)$ is real-valued. Hence, it is often convenient to work with real-valued components of Zernike moments for image reconstruction. A modified expression for the inverse moment transform given in Eq. (5.20) can be obtained as follows [100]. Using the property in Eq. (5.8), we can re-write Eq. (5.20) in terms of the real-valued polynomials R_{pq}.

$$f(r,\theta) \cong \sum_{p=0}^{n} \left\{ \frac{Z_{p0}^{(c)}}{2} R_{p0}(r,\theta) + \sum_{q>0}(Z_{pq}^{(c)} \cos q\theta + Z_{pq}^{(s)} \sin q\theta) R_{pq}(r,\theta) \right\}. \tag{5.21}$$

$Z_{pq}^{(c)}$, $Z_{pq}^{(s)}$ are the *real-valued Zernike moment components* given by

$$Z_{pq}^{(c)} = \frac{2(p+1)}{\pi} \int_{0}^{2\pi} \int_{0}^{1} R_{pq}(r,\theta) \ f(r,\theta) \ \cos q\theta \ r \ dr \ d\theta \quad , \quad q \ge 0,$$

$$Z_{pq}^{(s)} = \frac{-2(p+1)}{\pi} \int_{0}^{2\pi} \int_{0}^{1} R_{pq}(r,\theta) \ f(r,\theta) \ \sin q\theta \ r \ dr \ d\theta \quad , \quad q > 0. \tag{5.22}$$

We have the following relations between the above component functions and the actual Zernike moments Z_{pq}:

$$Z_{pq}^{(c)} = 2 \operatorname{Re}(Z_{pq}) ; \qquad Z_{pq}^{(s)} = -2 \operatorname{Im}(Z_{pq})$$

$$Z_{pq} = \frac{Z_{pq}^{(c)} - iZ_{pq}^{(s)}}{2} = Z_{p,-q}^{*} , \quad q > 0. \tag{5.23}$$

5.2 Zernike Moment Invariants

In this section, we derive functions of Zernike and Pseudo-Zernike moments which are invariants with respect to a rotational transform of the image. The large dynamic range of the invariants are further reduced by using a normalization procedure.

5.2.1 Rotation Invariants

From the definition of the Zernike moments as given in Eq. (5.1), it is easy to see that when an image undergoes a rotation by an angle α, the transformed moment functions Z'_{pq} are given by

$$Z'_{pq} = Z_{pq} e^{-iq\alpha} \quad . \tag{5.24}$$

From the above equation, the following invariant functions can be derived.

$$\varphi_1 = Z_{p0} ; \qquad \varphi_2 = |Z_{pq}|^2 . \tag{5.25}$$

The above invariants are often referred to as *primary invariants*. A more general expression for Zernike moment invariants is given by

$$\varphi_3 = (Z_{pq})^{*}(Z_{rs})^{m} + [(Z_{pq})^{*}(Z_{rs})^{m}]^{*} \tag{5.26}$$

where q is divisible by s, and, $m \geq 1$, $m = q/s$. The above type of invariants is referred to as *secondary invariants*. In Eq. (5.26), the term $Z_{pq}^{*} (Z_{rs})^{m}$ itself is an invariant, but the addition of its conjugate is done to get a real-valued invariant. A few rotation invariants and their corresponding expressions in geometric moments [see Eq.(5.19)] are given below as examples.

$$Z_{20} = (3/\pi) \ [2(m_{20} + m_{02}) - m_{00}]$$

$$|Z_{22}|^2 = (3/\pi)^2 \ [(m_{20} - m_{02})^2 + 4m_{11}^2]$$

$$|Z_{31}|^2 = (12/\pi)^2 \, [(m_{30} + m_{12})^2 + (m_{03} + m_{21})^2]$$

$$|Z_{33}|^2 = (4/\pi)^2 \, [(m_{30} - 3m_{12})^2 + (m_{03} - 3m_{21})^2]. \tag{5.27}$$

In the above equation, it is assumed that the origin of the coordinate system has already been shifted to the image centroid to achieve translation invariance, so that $m_{10} = m_{01} = 0$.

The pseudo-Zernike moments have also the same invariants of the type given in Eq. (5.25) and Eq. (5.26).

5.2.2 *Normalized Zernike Invariants*

The magnitudes of the Zernike moment invariants vary largely with the order of the moment functions; and to reduce the large dynamic range of invariants, the Zernike moments Z_{pq} are usually normalized to the functions $\hat{Z}_{pq}$, as follows [14]:

$$\hat{Z}_{pq} = Z_{pq} \, / \, Z_{p-2, \, q} \, , \qquad \text{if } Z_{p-2, \, q} \neq 0, \text{ and } q < p.$$

$$\hat{Z}_{pq} = Z_{pq} \, , \qquad \text{if } Z_{p-2, \, q} = 0, \text{ or } q = p. \tag{5.28}$$

The Pseudo-Zernike moments $\widetilde{Z}_{pq}$ are also similarly normalized to $\hat{\widetilde{Z}}_{pq}$ as given below.

$$\hat{\widetilde{Z}}_{pq} = \widetilde{Z}_{pq} \, / \, \widetilde{Z}_{p-1,q} \, , \qquad \text{if } \widetilde{Z}_{p-1,q} \neq 0, \text{ and } q < p$$

$$\hat{\widetilde{Z}}_{pq} = \widetilde{Z}_{pq} \, , \qquad \text{if } \widetilde{Z}_{p-1,q} = 0, \text{ or } q = p \, . \tag{5.29}$$

The normalized moments, $\hat{Z}_{pq}$, $\hat{\widetilde{Z}}_{pq}$ are used in the respective invariants to construct the feature vectors [see Section 7.1]. The reduced dynamic range makes it possible to use higher order moment invariants in pattern recognition applications, to achieve higher accuracy and recognition capability of the feature descriptors.

5.3 Fast Computation of Zernike Moments

We discuss below methods to reduce the amount of computation involved in the evaluation of Zernike moments of a gray-level image. The Zernike polynomials can be computed using recursive relations to eliminate factorial terms. Contour integration methods are adopted to minimize data storage and computation time for binary images. An image transformation suitable for generating moments in polar coordinates is also introduced to significantly reduce the computational overhead.

5.3.1 *Recursive Computation of Zernike Polynomials*

A recursive formula to compute the Zernike polynomials $R_{nm}(r)$ in terms of $R_{n-2, m}(r)$ and $R_{n+2,m}(r)$, is given in [103]. This formula, suitably modified for forward computation, is given below. The initial step for the recursive relation can be chosen as $R_{mm}(r) = r^m$.

$$R_{n,m}(r) = \frac{(k_2 r^2 + k_3)\, R_{n-2,m}(r) + k_4\, R_{n-4,m}(r)}{k_1} \,, \qquad (5.30)$$

where

$$k_1 = (n-1)\,(n+1)\,(n-2)\,/\,2\,,$$

$$k_2 = 2n\,(n-1)\,(n-2)\,,$$

$$k_3 = -\,(n-1)^3\,,$$

$$k_4 = -n\,(n-1)\,(n-3)\,/\,2\,.$$

It should be noted that the above method provides a recursive scheme over the index n only. The whole process will have to be repeated for a different value of m with the corresponding initial value. As an alternate way to compute the Zernike polynomials, the following recursive relations for the coefficients B_{pqk} of the radial polynomials can be derived from Eq. (5.11):

$$B_{ppp} = 1\,,$$

$$B_{p(q-2)p} = B_{pqp}\,\frac{(p+q)}{(p-q+2)} \,,$$

$$B_{pq(s-2)} = B_{pqs} \frac{q^2 - s^2}{(p+s)(p-s+2)}.$$ (5.31)

The flow-chart for the computation of Zernike polynomials using the above equations is shown in Fig. 5.1.

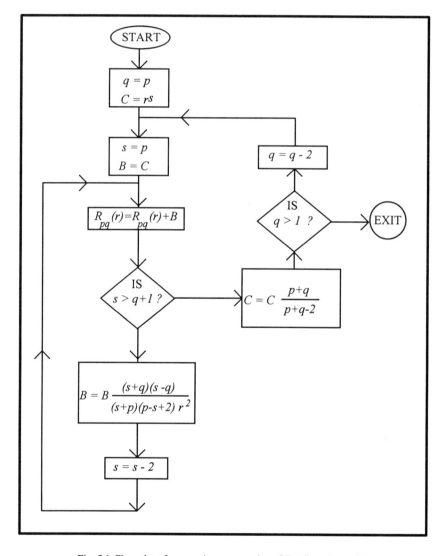

Fig. 5.1 Flow-chart for recursive computation of Zernike polynomials.

5.3.2 *Contour Integration of Zernike Moments*

A fast method to evaluate the Zernike moments of a binary image, using contour integration along the boundary points of the image, is described below. In polar form, the boundary points of an image can be represented as $\{\, r_\theta : \quad 0 \leq \theta \leq 2\pi \,\}$, where r_θ denotes the radial distance to the boundary point situated at an angle θ. The boundary contour is assumed to be a non-intersecting closed curve, with the origin of the polar coordinate system located inside the bounded region. Using the series representation of the Zernike polynomial as in Eq. (5.10), the Zernike moments of order p can be expressed as

$$Z_{pq} = \frac{p+1}{\pi} \int_0^{2\pi} \left\{ \sum_{k=m}^{n} B_{nmk} \int_0^{r_\theta} r^{k+1}\, dr \right\} e^{-jm\theta} d\theta\,. \tag{5.32}$$

The above expression further reduces to the following discrete form:

$$Z_{pq} = \frac{p+1}{\pi} \sum_{k=m}^{n} \left(\frac{B_{nmk}}{k+2} \right) \sum_{\theta=0}^{2\pi} \left\{ r_\theta^{k+2} (\cos m\theta - i \sin m\theta) \right\} \Delta\theta\,, \tag{5.33}$$

where $\Delta\theta$ is the incremental angle between successive boundary points. If the image boundary points are denoted by the set $\{(r_i\,,\ \theta_i\,)\,,\ i{=}1,2...N\}$, where N is the total number of boundary points, then Eq. (5.33) can also be written as

$$Z_{pq} = \frac{p+1}{\pi} \sum_{k=m}^{n} \left(\frac{B_{nmk}}{k+2} \right) \sum_{i=1}^{N} \left\{ r_i^{k+2} (\cos m\theta_i - i \sin m\theta_i) \right\}(\theta_{i+1} - \theta_i) \tag{5.34}$$

5.3.3 *Square-to-Circular Image Transform*

Since Zernike moments are defined in terms of polar coordinates (r,θ), the Zernike polynomials will have to be evaluated at each pixel position, and the computations involved are significantly large compared to Legendre moments and geometric moments. The polar form of Zernike moments suggests a square-to-circular image transformation, so that the Zernike polynomials need be computed only once for all pixels mapped to the same circle. The Zernike moments thus computed, though differ from the true moments of the rectangular image, can be used as feature descriptors for image identification and reconstruction applications. The procedure for the transformation of the pixel space from a square region to a circular region is schematically shown in Fig. 5.2 below. With reference to Fig. 5.2, the image pixels can be thought of as arranged along concentric squares and can be mapped to concentric circles by the following transformation. If the image coordinate system (x, y) is defined with the origin at the center of the square pixel grid, then the pixel coordinates of the transformed circular image can be represented by two numbers γ, ξ where γ denotes the radius of the circle and ξ the position index of the pixel on the circle.

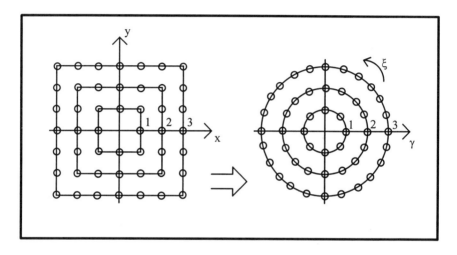

Fig. 5.3 Schematic of square-to-circular image transformation.

The integral values of γ, ξ can be obtained as follows:

$$\gamma = \text{maximum } \{ |x|, |y| \},$$

If $|x| = \gamma$, then $\xi = 2 (\gamma-x)\dfrac{y}{|y|} + \dfrac{xy}{\gamma}.$

If $|y| = \gamma$, then $\xi = 2 y - \dfrac{xy}{\gamma}.$ (5.35)

The above transformation, albeit non-linear, is one-to-one and invertible. It is also assumed that the image intensity values are preserved under the transformation, so that $f(x, y) = f(\gamma, \xi)$.   If N denotes the image size in pixels, then the ranges of values of the coordinate indices are given by

$$-N/2 \le x, y \le N/2; \qquad 0 \le \gamma \le N/2; \qquad 1 \le \xi \le 8\gamma. \qquad (5.36)$$

The normalized polar coordinates r, θ of the pixel (γ, ξ) are given by

$$r = 2\gamma/N,$$

$$\theta = \pi\xi/(4\gamma). \qquad (5.37)$$

Also, $dr = 2/N$, and $d\theta = \pi/(4\gamma)$, so that

$$r\, dr\, d\theta = \pi/N^2. \qquad (5.38)$$

5.3.4 Computation of Zernike Moments of Gray-level Images

In this section, we discuss a fast algorithm to compute the Zernike moments of a gray-level image, using the square-to-circular image transform given in the previous section. The real-valued Zernike moment components in Eq. (5.22) can be written in the discrete form using the coordinates of the transformed circular image with the help of Eqs. (5.37), (5.38) as

$$Z_{pq}^{(c)} = \frac{2p+2}{N^2} \sum_{\gamma=1}^{N/2} R_{pq}\left(\frac{2\gamma}{N}\right) \sum_{\xi=1}^{8\gamma} \cos\left(\frac{\pi q\xi}{4\gamma}\right) f(r,\theta),$$

$$Z_{pq}^{(s)} = \frac{-(2p+2)}{N^2} \sum_{\gamma=1}^{N/2} R_{pq}\left(\frac{2\gamma}{N}\right) \sum_{\xi=1}^{8\gamma} \sin\left(\frac{\pi q\xi}{4\gamma}\right) f(r,\theta). \qquad (5.39)$$

From the above equations, it is clear that the Zernike polynomials R_{pq} need be evaluated only $N/2$ times for a circular image, as against N^2 times for a normal square image. This reduction in the number of polynomial evaluation leads to a considerable saving in computational time needed for Zernike moment calculations.

5.4 Conclusions

Zernike moments are complex, orthogonal moment descriptors which find potential applications in pattern recognition. Zernike moments have superior feature representation capabilities and are more robust in the presence of image noise, compared to other types of moment functions. The kernel of Zernike moments are defined in terms of the radial Zernike polynomials. The properties of Zernike polynomials, and pseudo-Zernike polynomials have been detailed. Recursive algorithms to evaluate Zernike polynomials are given. A contour integration method to evaluate Zernike moments of binary images is presented. A fast method using a square-to-circular image transform, to compute the Zernike moments of gray-level images is also given.

References

- **Definitions and Properties**: [8], [16], [19], [65], [66], [67], [81], [82], [100], [101], [103], [146], [152], [153], [155], [170], [177], [182], [196], [209], [225].

- **Zernike Moment Invariants**: [14], [15], [96], [97], [99], [100], [102], [148], [155], [159], [196], [199].

- **Fast Computation of Zernike Moments**: [141], [142].

Chapter 6
Moment Tensors

The fundamental advantage of geometric moments over other types of moments considered so far, is that a general linear transformation of an image can be directly translated into a corresponding transformation in the moment feature space. The transformation of geometric moments satisfy the properties of a contravariant relative tensor, which help in further exploring the characteristics of geometric moments viewed as tensors.

Tensors provide an elegant mathematical structure for analyzing the behavior of moments under various two-dimensional image plane transformations. Expressions for geometric moment invariants can also be obtained by constructing appropriate tensor invariants. Moment tensors have been used in several applications such as three dimensional object attitude estimation [42], pattern matching under affine transformations [48], and the generation of high dimensional moment invariants [129].

6.1 Mathematical Preliminaries

Some important concepts in tensor theory are recalled in this section, as a pre-requisite to developing the mathematical framework of moment tensors. Though tensors are generally defined in an n-dimensional space, the following discussion will consider only the two dimensional space spanned by an orthogonal set of unit vectors (e_1, e_2).

6.1.1 *Tensors and Linear Transformations*

We denote a vector in two-dimensional metric space by $x = (x^1, x^2)$, where x^i are the components (coordinates), and the superscripts (and subscripts) denote the axis indices and not the powers. In the usual Cartesian notation, x^1 represents the x-coordinate, and x^2 the y-coordinate. The base-vectors (unit vectors) along the coordinate axes are denoted by e_i, i=1,2; so that

$$x = x^i e_i .\tag{6.1}$$

In the above equation, the convention of Einstein summation is used, where it is understood that the components are summed over repeated indices.

A general linear transformation $x \to y$ of the coordinate system can be represented in the form

$$T: \quad y^i = a^i_j x_j, \qquad i{=}1,2 \tag{6.2}$$

where a^i_j are the elements of the transformation matrix. T is called an *affine transformation*, if $|a^i_j|$ does not vanish, so that T^{-1} exists and is single-valued. The Jacobian of the transformation is

$$J = \left| \frac{\partial y^i}{\partial x^j} \right| = |a^i_j|. \tag{6.3}$$

Consider a set of functions, $A^{j_1,j_2,...j_s}_{i_1,i_2,....i_r}(x)$ where each index takes values 1 or 2. The symbol A therefore represents 2^{r+s} functions. Under the coordinate transformation (6.1), these functions also get transformed to a set of functions, say, $B^{j_1,j_2,...j_s}_{i_1,i_2,....i_r}(y)$.

The totality of sets of 2^{r+s} functions, typified in the x coordinate system by the expressions A, is called a *mixed tensor*, covariant of rank r, contravariant of rank s, provided

$$B^{j_1,j_2,...j_s}_{i_1,i_2,...i_r}(y) = \frac{\partial x^{\alpha_1}}{\partial y^{i_1}} \frac{\partial x^{\alpha_2}}{\partial y^{i_2}} \cdots \frac{\partial x^{\alpha_r}}{\partial y^{i_r}} \frac{\partial y^{j_1}}{\partial x^{\beta_1}} \frac{\partial y^{j_2}}{\partial x^{\beta_2}} \cdots \frac{\partial y^{j_s}}{\partial x^{\beta_s}} \left| \frac{\partial x^j}{\partial y^j} \right|^\omega A^{\beta_1,\beta_2,...\beta_s}_{\alpha_1,\alpha_2,...\alpha_r}(x) \tag{6.4}$$

where ω is an integer. If $\omega{=}0$, the tensor is an *absolute tensor*, and otherwise it is called a *relative tensor* of weight ω. The indices i_1, i_2,...i_r are referred to as *covariant indices*, and $j_1,j_2,...j_s$ are the *contravariant indices*.

$A^{j_1,j_2,...j_s}_{i_1,i_2,...i_r}(x)$ is called the component of the tensor in the frame x, and the totality of 2^{r+s} functions represent the components of A. If the interchange two covariant or contravariant indices in the components does not alter its value, then the tensor is called a *symmetric tensor*. If the value changes by sign for an odd permutation of the indices, and if the value is unaltered for an even permutation of the indices, then the tensor is called *skew symmetric*.

If all components of a tensor vanish in one coordinate system, then they necessarily vanish in all the other coordinate systems. If a tensor is symmetric in one system, then it is so in all the other systems. The value of any skew-symmetric tensor with repeated indices is necessarily zero.

6.1.2 *The ε-Systems and Kronecker Deltas*

In an n-dimensional space, a skew-symmetric tensor is called an ε-system if its value is $+1$ when the indices are an even permutation of $1,2,...n$; and its value is -1 for an odd permutation of the indices. Being skew-symmetric, its value is 0, when two or more indices are repeated. In the two-dimensional case, we have

$$\varepsilon^{12} = \varepsilon_{12} = 1; \qquad \varepsilon^{21} = \varepsilon_{21} = -1. \tag{6.5}$$

ε_{ij} are relative tensors of weight -1, and ε^{ij} are relative tensors of weight 1.

The generalized Kronecker delta is denoted by $\delta^{j_1,j_2,...j_k}_{i_1,i_2,.....i_k}$, and this system contains k subscripts and k superscripts. The system is completely skew-symmetric in subscripts and superscripts. If the subscripts and superscripts are same with only a difference in the order, then δ has a value $+1$ for an even permutation, and -1 for an odd permutation. In all other cases, the system has a value 0. Generalized Kronecker deltas are absolute tensors.

6.1.3 *Tensor Operations*

The tensor operations required to derive moment invariants are briefly outlined below.

1. *Contraction*: In $A^{j_1,j_2,...j_s}_{i_1,i_2,.....i_r}(x)$, if we equate a covariant index and a contravariant index, and sum with respect to that index, then the resulting set of 2^{r+s-2} functions is a mixed tensor of covariant rank $r-1$, and contravariant rank $s-1$. This tensor is called a contraction of A. Note that one of the repeated index must be a subscript and the other a superscript. Thus only mixed tensors can be contracted.

2. *Outer product*: The set of quantities consisting of the product of each element of the set $A^{j_1,j_2,...j_s}_{i_1,i_2,.....i_r}(x)$ representing tensor A , by each element of the set $B^{l_1,l_2,...l_q}_{k_1,k_2,.k_p}(x)$

representing tensor B , defines another tensor C of covariant rank $p+r$, and contravariant rank $q+s$. This tensor is called the outer product of A and B, and

$$C_{i_1,i_2,\ldots,i_r,k_1,k_2,\ldots k_p}^{j_1,j_2,\ldots,j_s,l_1,l_2,\ldots l_q}(x) = A_{i_1,i_2,\ldots,i_r}^{j_1,j_2,\ldots j_s}(x)\ B_{k_1,k_2,\ldots k_p}^{l_1,l_2,\ldots l_q}(x)\ . \tag{6.6}$$

3. *Inner product*: It is possible to apply the operation of contraction to the outer product of two tensors. The resulting tensor is called the inner product of the two tensors. For example,

$$C_i^{jl} = A_i^{jk} B_k^l\ . \tag{6.7}$$

4. *Alternation*: The inner product of a tensor with an ε-system is called an alternation of the tensor. For example,

$$B^{klmn} = \varepsilon_{ij} A^{klijmn}\ . \tag{6.8}$$

6.2 Application of Tensor Theory to Geometric Moments

In tensor notation, the $(p+q)^{\text{th}}$ order geometric moments given in Eq. (2.1) are given by

$$m_{pq} = T^{ij\cdots} = \int\int x^i\, x^j \ldots\, f(x^1, x^2)\, dx^1\, dx^2\ , \qquad i, j = 1,2. \tag{6.9}$$

where a total of p indices among $i, j, \ldots$ have the value 1, and a total of q indices have the value 2. The tensor representation of moments up to the third order are given below.

Zero-order moment: $m_{00} = T$

First-order moments: $m_{10} = T^1;\quad m_{01} = T^2$

Second-order moments: $m_{20} = T^{11};\quad m_{11} = T^{12};\quad m_{02} = T^{22}$

Third-order moments: $m_{30} = T^{111};\quad m_{21} = T^{112};\quad m_{12} = T^{122};\quad m_{03} = T^{222}$

$$\tag{6.10}$$

In the following section, we show that $T^{ij\cdots}$ is indeed a tensor.

6.2.1 *Tensor Characteristics of Geometric Moments*

Consider the general linear transformation in (6.2) which can be put in the matrix form as

$$
\begin{bmatrix} y^1 \\ y^2 \end{bmatrix} = \begin{bmatrix} a_1^1 & a_2^1 \\ a_1^2 & a_2^2 \end{bmatrix} \begin{bmatrix} x^1 \\ x^2 \end{bmatrix}
\tag{6.11}
$$

where a_j^i are constants and $|a_j^i| \neq 0$. Let $\overline{T}^{ij\cdots}$ denote the transformed moments under the coordinate transformation (6.11). Then,

$$
\overline{T}^{ij\cdots} = \int\!\int y^i y^j \cdots f(y^1, y^2) \, dy^1 \, dy^2 , \qquad i,j = 1,2.
\tag{6.12}
$$

On substituting for y's from Eq. (6.11) and noting that

$$
dy^1 \, dy^2 = \left| \frac{\partial y^i}{\partial x^j} \right| dx^1 \, dx^2 ,
\tag{6.13}
$$

we get

$$
\overline{T}^{ij\cdots} = a_k^i \, a_l^j \cdots \left| \frac{\partial x^i}{\partial y^j} \right|^{-1} \int\!\int x^k x^l \cdots f(x^1, x^2) \, dx^1 \, dx^2 , \qquad i,j = 1,2.
\tag{6.14}
$$

i.e.,

$$
\overline{T}^{ij\cdots} = \frac{\partial y^i}{\partial x^k} \frac{\partial y^j}{\partial x^l} \cdots \left| \frac{\partial x^i}{\partial y^j} \right|^{-1} T^{kl\cdots} .
\tag{6.15}
$$

The above equation shows that $T^{ij\cdots}$ (and hence, m_{pq}) is a relative tensor of weight -1, and contravariant rank $p+q$. Further, $T^{ij\cdots}$ is a symmetric tensor. In obtaining Eq. (6.15), we have also assumed that the transformation preserves the image intensity distribution, so that $f(y^1, y^2) = f(x^1, x^2)$.

The term $\left| \dfrac{\partial x^i}{\partial y^j} \right|^{-1}$ can be eliminated from Eq. (6.15) by noting that

$$\overline{T} = \left| \frac{\partial x^i}{\partial y^j} \right|^{-1} T \, .$$

(6.16)

Hence, the functions $T^{ij\cdots}/T$ (i.e., m_{pq}/m_{00}) are absolute symmetric tensors of contravariant rank $p+q$.

If we restrict object transformations to only rotations, then the transformation matrix is orthonormal and the Jacobian is unity. With these conditions, there is no difference between the covariant and contravariant components of a tensor (i.e., $A^{ij\cdots} = A_{ij\cdots}$), and the moment tensors become absolute Cartesian tensors.

6.2.2 Derivation of Moment Tensor Invariants

An algebraic invariant of a tensor A is an integral rational homogeneous function $\mathfrak{I}$ of its components $A^{j_1,j_2,\ldots j_s}_{i_1,i_2,\ldots i_r}(x)$, which transforms as

$$\mathfrak{I}(B) = \Delta^w \, \mathfrak{I}(A)$$

(6.17)

under the tensor transformation in Eq. (6.4). In the above equation, Δ is the determinant of the transformation, and w is the weight of the invariant. The order of the invariant is the sum of the powers in any of its terms. We construct an tensor invariant by using the following theorem [129].

Theorem on tensor invariants : An algebraic invariant of a weight w and order d can be constructed from a tensor A by $d-1$ multiplications and w alternations.

We show below the construction of an invariant from the second-order moment tensor m^{ij}. An invariant of order 2 and weight 2 can be constructed by two alternations of the product $m^{ij} m^{kl}$ such as

$$\mathfrak{I}(m) = \varepsilon_{ik} \, \varepsilon_{jp} \, m^{ij} \, m^{kp},$$

(6.18)

which after performing the summation over repeated indices become

$$\mathfrak{I}(m) = 2 \, [\, m^{11} \, m^{22} - (m^{12})^2 \,] \, .$$

(6.19)

In standard notation of geometric moments, the above invariant is written as

$$\varphi = m_{20}\, m_{02} + m_{11}^{2}. \tag{6.20}$$

The multiplication factor 2 in Eq. (6.19) is omitted in the above expression, being a constant.

6.2.3 Derivation of Unit Rank Tensors

Unit rank tensors T^{k} have a very simple transformation rule given by [see Eq.(6.14)]

$$\overline{T}^{i} = a_{k}^{i}\, T^{k}. \tag{6.21}$$

The above equation is linear in the elements of the attitude transformation matrix given in Eq.(6.11), and is therefore useful in solving for these elements in object pose estimation problems. Independent equations of type (6.21) can be derived by reducing moment tensors of different orders to unit rank tensors. If S^{ijk} denotes a third order moment and F^{ijkl} denotes a fourth order moment, then a unit tensor F^{l} can be obtained by a simple contraction among the indices of the two tensors S and F as follows:

$$F^{l} = F^{ijkl}\, S^{ijk} \tag{6.22}$$

The application of unit tensors in attitude estimation problems is described in Section 8.2.3.

6.3 Conclusions

The properties of geometric moments viewed as components of a contravariant tensor, are described. Tensors provide a suitable framework for analyzing the behavior of moments under image transformations. Under orthogonal coordinate transformations, the moments behave as absolute tensors. The mathematical preliminaries on tensor operations and tensor invariants have been outlined. The theorem on tensor invariants has been used to derive geometric moment invariants.

References

- **Mathematical Preliminaries**: [13], [41], [43], [44], [129].

- **Application of Tensor Theory to Geometric Moments**: [11], [13], [42], [48], [129], [150], [203].

PART 2

Moment Functions - Applications

Chapter 7
Pattern Recognition and Object Identification

The shape representation characteristics of moment functions have been effectively used in recognizing object features from images. Important application areas of moment based features are pattern recognition, optical character recognition, object identification and classification. The invariant functions of geometric and orthogonal moments can be utilized for distortion invariant recognition of shapes.

The most common method adopted in moment based recognition algorithms is the comparison of feature vectors of a set of reference images with the given image of an unknown object. The feature vectors are constituted by invariant functions of moments of different orders, so that the global shape characteristics of the image are available with the required level of detail, and at the same time are invariant with respect to camera position and rotation angle.

7.1 Feature Representation

The moment features computed from images can be used to identify the object, irrespective of the position and orientation of the image in its plane. A set of moment functions of a particular image is referred to as a feature vector. A set of feature vectors can be used to represent a class of patterns, or a set of different views of an object. This section describes the various methods of defining feature vectors, for the purposes of matching global shape parameters of images.

7.1.1 *Feature Vector Selection*

The selection of an appropriate feature vector for a particular pattern matching application, is generally based on the following aspects:

1. *Information content*: The number and order of moments needed to adequately and unambiguously represent the shape features.

2. *Robustness* : Sensitivity of the components of feature vectors to image noise, spatial quantization, and intensity quantization.

3. *Information redundancy*: Capability of the components of feature vectors to characterize independent image features.

Moments of different orders usually exhibit large dynamic range variations. This leads to the domination of a subgroup of features among a set of moments. Therefore, the moments in a feature vector will have to be appropriately weighted to get a balanced representation of different components of the image shape. Higher order moments are more sensitive to image noise and quantization effects, and can lead to mismatches in pattern recognition algorithms. Moments of orders higher than four are not commonly used in feature vector construction. Orthogonal moments are less sensitive to noise compared to geometric moments, and have a higher degree of information content. Moments computed from an image are also sometimes combined with moments evaluated from the image boundary, to represent both minute details of shape as well as gross structural features.

7.1.2 *Feature Vector Matching*

The feature vector computed from an image (measurement) has to be compared and matched with a class of feature vectors stored a priori (reference), to establish the correspondence between the given image (of an unknown object or pattern) and a standard image (of a known object or pattern). We discuss below the different methods used in the construction and matching of moment feature vectors. Fig. 7.1 shows a schematic of a set of reference feature vectors.

Image (k)	Feature vector				
	1	2	3	......	n
1					
2					
:					
k	$v_1^{(k)}$	$v_2^{(k)}$	$v_3^{(k)}$		$v_n^{(k)}$
:					:

Fig. 7.1 Feature vector representation of images.

We denote a feature vector corresponding to an image k by

$$V^{(k)} = \{ v_1^{(k)}, v_2^{(k)}, v_3^{(k)}, \ldots\ldots v_n^{(k)} \} , \qquad (7.1)$$

where each component $v_i^{(k)}$ is typically an invariant moment function of the image. The set of all $V^{(k)}$'s constitute the reference library of feature vectors. The images for which the reference vectors are computed and stored as above are either a set of patterns (used for pattern recognition) or different views of a three-dimensional object (used for object identification). The problem considered here is to match a feature vector

$$V' = \{ v_1', v_2', v_3', \ldots\ldots v_n' \} \qquad (7.2)$$

of the image of an unknown pattern or object view, with the vectors in the reference library to identify the pattern or view direction. The most common methods used in moment based feature vector matching algorithms are described below.

1. *Weighted Euclidean distance measure*:

$$d(V', V^{(k)}) = \sqrt{\sum_{i=1}^{n} \rho_i (v_i' - v_i^{(k)})^2} , \qquad (7.3)$$

where ρ_i denotes the weight added to the component v_i to balance the variations in the dynamic range. The value of k for which the function d is minimum, is selected as the matched image index. The inverse of the variance of the column $v_i^{(k)}$ is frequently used as the weight ρ_i, i.e.,

$$\rho_i = \frac{N}{\sum_{k=1}^{N} (v_i^{(k)} - \bar{v}_i)^2} , \qquad (7.4)$$

where

$$\bar{v}_i = \frac{\sum_{k=1}^{N} v_i^{(k)}}{N} . \qquad (7.5)$$

2. *Correlation coefficient method*:

The cross-correlation between the vectors V', $V^{(k)}$ is defined as

$$r\,(V', V^{(k)}) = \frac{\sum_{i=1}^{n} v_i^{(k)} v_i{}'}{\left|\sum_{i=1}^{n}(v_i^{(k)})^2\right|^{1/2} \left|\sum_{i=1}^{n}(v_i{}')^2\right|^{1/2}} \cdot \qquad (7.6)$$

The value of k which makes r closest to 1 is chosen as the matched image index.

3. *Logarithmic magnitude distance measure*:

$$l(V', V^{(k)}) = \sqrt{\sum_{i=1}^{n}(\log|v_i{}'| - \log|v_i^{(k)}|)^2} \ . \qquad (7.7)$$

The logarithm of feature vector components are taken when there is a large dynamic range variation, as in the case of geometric moments of different orders.

4. *Minimum mean distance rule*:

The mean value $v_0^{(k)}$ of each feature vector is computed as

$$v_0^{(k)} = \frac{\sum_{i=1}^{n} v_i^{(k)}}{n} \ . \qquad (7.8)$$

and the Euclidean distance measure is applied as in Eq. (7.3), with $v_0^{(k)}$ in place of $v_i^{(k)}$; and the weights ρ_i computed as in (7.4).

5. *Statistical measure* using minimum and maximum:

The statistical measure compares the minimum and maximum values among the observation $v_i{}'$ and the reference $v_i^{(k)}$ and selects the vector which has minimum difference between the *Min* and *Max* values.

$$s_k = \sum_{i=1}^{n} \left[\frac{Max(v_i^{(k)}, v_i')}{Min(v_i^{(k)}, v_i')} - 1 \right]^2 . \tag{7.9}$$

The value of k which minimizes s_k is selected as the matched image index.

7.2 Image Normalization

The methods described in the previous section are generally used with moment invariants as feature vector components, so that each vector $V^{(k)}$ represents a shape in the image, irrespective of its orientation, position and scale factor. Another approach in matching shapes is to first transform the image to a standard image, and then compare the shape descriptors (which need not be invariants) of the standard (normalized) image with a reference library of descriptors stored a priori for a set of standard shapes. The process of transforming the image to a standard shape of predetermined attributes is called image normalization.

7.2.1 *Image Normalization Using Geometric Moments*

The normalization of an image using geometric moments involves transforming the image to a standard image having the following properties. (We denote the geometric moments of the standard image as $m_{pq}^{(s)}$).

$m_{00}^{(s)} = \beta$ (The total area is β, and the intensity values are 1)

$m_{10}^{(s)} = m_{01}^{(s)} = 0$ (The centroid of the shape is at the origin)

$m_{11}^{(s)} = 0$ (The reference axes are the principal axes)

$m_{20}^{(s)} \geq m_{02}^{(s)}$ (Major principal axis is the x-axis)

$m_{30}^{(s)} > 0$ (The projection onto the x-axis has negative skew)

$$\tag{7.10}$$

The first condition introduces scale normalization, the second gives translation normalization, and the remaining conditions yield rotation normalization.

If m_{pq} denote the geometric moments of the image to be normalized, then the following steps describe the normalization procedure:

Step 1: Transform the image coordinates from (x, y) to (x', y') such that

$$x' = \left(x - \frac{m_{10}}{m_{00}}\right)\sqrt{\frac{\beta}{m_{00}}} \quad ,$$

$$y' = \left(y - \frac{m_{01}}{m_{00}}\right)\sqrt{\frac{\beta}{m_{00}}} \quad . \tag{7.11}$$

The transformed image now obeys the first two conditions in (7.10).

Step 2: Compute the second order moments m_{pq}' of the transformed image, and obtain the principal axis orientation θ as

$$\theta = \frac{1}{2}\tan^{-1}\left(\frac{2m_{11}'}{m_{20}' - m_{02}'}\right) \tag{7.12}$$

Transform the image coordinates from (x', y') to (x'', y'') as follows, to align the principal axes with the coordinate reference axes:

$$x'' = x' \cos\theta + y' \sin\theta,$$

$$y'' = -x' \sin\theta + y' \cos\theta. \tag{7.13}$$

The transformed image now obeys the first four conditions in (7.10).

Step 3: Compute the third-order moment m_{30}'' of the above transformed image. (The superscripts $''$ are used only to denote the moments of the twice transformed image)

If $m_{30}'' < 0$, then rotate the image coordinate axes by 180 degrees. The transformed image now satisfies all the conditions in (7.10), and is in the standard form.

After normalizing the image, feature descriptors which are not necessarily invariants with respect to rotation, translation and scale variation (e.g., Legendre moments, Zernike moments) can be used in the construction of feature vectors, and the classification rules described in Section 7.1.2 applied.

7.2.2   *Image Normalization Using Complex Moments*

The normalization scheme described above uses moments of orders up to three only. A more general normalization method using higher order complex image moments was proposed by Abu-Mostafa [1]. The first four conditions in (7.10) are equivalent to the following conditions in the complex moments C_{pq}. [Eq.(3.29), Section 3.3]:

$C_{00} = \beta,$

$C_{10} = 0,$

C_{20} is positive real. $\qquad\qquad$ (7.14)

The above normalization scheme is called 'N_{20} normalization' [1]. In general, the normalization scheme which imposes the conditions,

$C_{00} = \beta,$

$C_{10} = 0,$

$C_{11} = \alpha$

C_{pq} is positive real, $\qquad\qquad$ (7.15)

where α, β are positive real constants; is called N_{pq} *normalization*. Since C_{pq} is the complex conjugate of C_{qp} [Eq. (3.31)], N_{pq} is equivalent to N_{qp} . This redundancy can be eliminated by imposing the constraint $p > q$. From Eq. (3.32), we find that C_{pq} will become positive real at angles equally spaced at $2\pi/(p-q)$ radians apart, and hence N_{pq} has a degeneracy of $p-q$, and is not unique unless $p=1+q$.

7.3 Neural Networks

Artificial neural networks with their inherent parallelism are ideally suited to image processing. The neural nets are composed of many single non-linear computational elements (neurons) which are connected by links with variable weights. These processing elements operate in parallel, and the weights are selected to obtain the desired outputs. Neural nets provide a greater degree of robustness and fault tolerance than conventional computers, because of the many processing nodes; each of which is responsible for a small portion of the task. Damage to a few nodes or links does not impair the overall performance significantly.

Neural networks have been used in classifying patterns and identifying objects from images. This chapter presents neural network classifiers which use moment functions as inputs. The neural networks are trained with feature vectors with moment invariant components to obtain the desired classification index at the output. The most frequently used networks for the above application are multi-layer perceptrons, and the classification schemes are implemented using back-propagation algorithms. A brief description of these concepts is given below.

7.3.1 *Multi-layer Perceptron*

The multi-layer perceptron (MLP) is a network topology consisting of a feed-forward scheme, with one or more layers of nodes between the input and the output nodes. These in-between layers are called *hidden layers*. Each node in a layer is connected to all nodes in the layer above it. A MLP with one hidden layer is shown in Fig. 7.2.

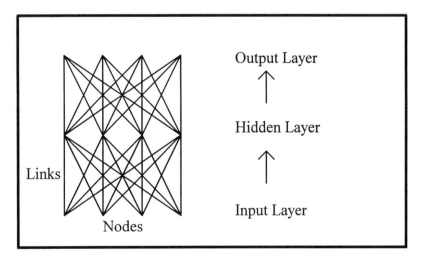

Fig. 7.2 A multi-layer perceptron with one hidden layer.

Each node j in the network is characterized by a threshold or offset k_j, and a non-linear function $f(.)$. The function f is sometimes referred to as the activation function of the neuron. The non-linearity is typically a *sigmoid function*. Each input x_i to a node is weighted by a factor w_i, and the sum of all weighted inputs is passed through the non-linearity, to generate the output y_j of the node as

$$y_j = f\left(\sum_{i=1}^{n_j} w_i x_i - k_j\right).$$ (7.16)

The sigmoid function $f(x)$ is given by

$$f(x) = \frac{1}{1+e^{-x}},$$ (7.17)

and a plot of this function is given in Fig. 7.3.

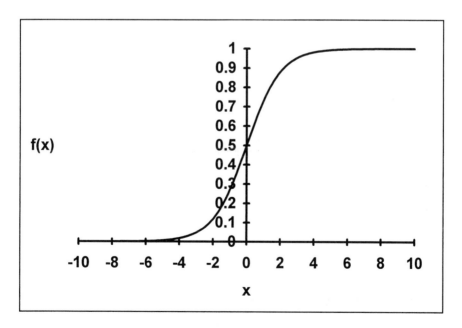

Fig. 7.3 Sigmoid function.

7.3.2 Back-Propagation Algorithm

The back-propagation algorithm gives a prescription for changing the weights of the neural net, by training the network by a given set of input-output pairs. Starting with an arbitrary set of values for the weights and node offsets, the input data are fed into the neural net to produce its own output data. This output is compared with the desired output, resulting in an error signal for each output unit. Weights are then adjusted to decrease the difference between the network output and the desired output. The back-propagation algorithm involves the following steps [121]:

Step 1: Set all weights and node offsets to small random values.

Step 2: Present the input vector elements v_i . Specify the desired output. Since the neural net is used as a classifier, the desired output is a value of 1 at the kth node, indicating that the input corresponds to an image with index k; and the values at all other output nodes are 0.

Step 3: Compute the outputs y_j at each node j. Find an error term δ_j for all the nodes as described below. If d_j is the desired output, and y_j is the actual output of the node j, then for an output node

$$\delta_j = (d_j - y_j) y_j (1 - y_j), \tag{7.18}$$

and for a hidden node

$$\delta_j = y_j (1 - y_j) \sum_i \delta_i w_i , \tag{7.19}$$

where i is over all nodes in the layer above node j, and w_i are the weights of the links from node j to the nodes in the layer above it.

Step 4: Adjust the weights by

$$w_i \leftarrow w_i + \alpha \, \delta_j \, y_i \tag{7.20}$$

and repeat from step 2.

The above procedure is only the basic algorithm, and further analysis and refinements needed for fast convergence of the weights are given in [121].

In order to classify patterns using moment functions, a feature vector $V^{(k)}$ of the type given in Eq. (7.1) is presented at the input, and the output is specified as the value of the output node k being 1, and the remaining values 0. The feature vector consists of moment invariants. The neural network is trained using the back-propagation algorithm, and with different images represented by the same feature vector (i.e., images which are scaled, translated and rotated versions of the original image), specifying the same output. After the weights have converged, the network training procedure is repeated with another input-output pair. The role of the neural networks of the type described above, is to act as a classifier. A suitable set of moment invariants is extracted from the patterns selected for classification, and this set of invariants is presented at the input of the network, whose purpose is to partition the space of features into decision regions corresponding to each pattern class. A different class of neural networks where the moment invariants are directly incorporated in the structure of the dynamics of the neural network is presented in Perantonis [148]. Here the input is simply the image intensity values and the output is the desired pattern class.

7.4 Conclusions

Pattern recognition and object identification are the most important and frequently found applications of moment functions. The capability of moment invariants to represent image shapes irrespective of their rotation, translation and scale variation, has been effectively used to construct feature vectors, and to identify an image by feature vector correspondence. Another method for object classification is by normalizing an image to a standard shape using geometric moments. A generalization of the image normalization scheme using higher order complex moments is also described. A brief description of the neural network implementation consisting of a multi-layer perceptron with back-propagation training algorithm, is also given. This type of neural networks is commonly used as pattern classifiers, with moment invariant feature vector as input.

References

- **Feature Representation and Classification**: [8], [10], [11], [14], [27], [32], [39], [47], [50], [55], [61], [68], [73], [74], [75], [76], [78], [81], [85], [88], [89], [96], [99], [100], [102], [107], [124], [130], [135], [147], [151], [158], [176], [180], [182], [188], [201], [203], [206], [210], [216], [217], [218].

- **Image Normalization**: [1], [30], [63], [96], [100], [166], [167], [170].

- **Neural Networks**: [37], [54], [74], [97], [98], [121], [143], [148], [159], [171], [192], [219], [223].

Chapter 8
Attitude and Position Estimation

We have seen that moment functions can represent shape features of an image. Moment functions can also be used to represent image plane transformations by a corresponding set of transformations in the moment space. The moments computed from both the initial and transformed images can be related through a set of projection equations involving the three-dimensional position and orientation parameters of the object. These moment equations obtained for different orders of moments, can be solved for the unknown parameters, to recover the object pose (attitude and position) information.

8.1 2D Object Pose Recovery

The 2D object pose recovery refers to the problem of estimating the object position and orientation, where the rotation is constrained to be in a plane parallel to the image plane. With the above constraint, the object motion directly corresponds to a rotation, translation and scale variation in the image plane. These parameters can be derived using the geometric moments up to the second order, of the initial and transformed images.

The position of the object is defined with respect to camera-fixed frame (X,Y,Z), and the 2D rotation parallel to the image-plane is defined with respect to the angle θ measured from the u-axis of the image reference frame (Fig. 8.1).

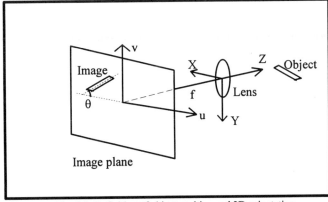

Fig. 8.1 Definition of object position and 2D-orientation.

Let the initial position and orientation of the object be (X,Y,Z), θ ; and let the corresponding parameters of the transformed configuration of the object be (X',Y',Z'), θ'. If m_{ij} , m'_{ij} denote the moments of the initial and transformed images in the pixel coordinate space (u, v), then

$$m_{00} = \iint du\, dv = (f^2/Z^2) \iint dX\, dY,$$

$$m'_{00} = \iint du'\, dv' = (f^2/Z'^2) \iint dX'\, dY',$$

$$m_{10}/m_{00} = Xf/Z; \qquad\qquad m'_{10}/m_{00} = X'f/Z',$$

$$m_{01}/m_{00} = Xf/Z; \qquad\qquad m'_{01}/m_{00} = Y'f/Z'. \qquad (8.1)$$

where, f denotes the focal length of the camera. From the above expressions, it is easy to derive the following equations which give the final object position in terms of the initial position and the image moments.

$$Z' = Z\sqrt{\frac{m_{00}}{m'_{00}}}\ ,$$

$$X' = X\frac{m'_{10}}{m_{10}}\sqrt{\frac{m_{00}}{m'_{00}}}\ ,$$

$$Y' = Y\frac{m'_{01}}{m_{01}}\sqrt{\frac{m_{00}}{m'_{00}}}\ . \qquad (8.2)$$

The relative orientation between the initial and final configurations can be obtained by using their respective central moments μ_{ij} and μ'_{ij} , and Eq. (2.15) :

$$\theta' - \theta = \frac{1}{2}\tan^{-1}\frac{2[\mu'_{11}(\mu_{20} - \mu_{02}) - \mu_{11}(\mu'_{20} - \mu'_{02})]}{(\mu_{20} - \mu_{02})(\mu'_{20} - \mu'_{02}) - 4\mu'_{11}\mu_{11}}. \qquad (8.3)$$

8.2 3D Object Pose Recovery

We consider here the problem of estimating the general three-dimensional orientation and position parameters of an object from its image moments. A three-dimensional rotation of an object does not always have a direct mapping to a corresponding transformation in the image plane, due to surface occlusions. This problem is circumvented by either (i) by using a planar feature pattern on the object which is assumed to be completely visible in the image throughout the object motion, or (ii) by constructing a library of views of the object taken from several directions, and using this set to identify an unknown view direction. The above two methods are analyzed in this chapter.

8.2.1 *Pose Estimation Using Planar Feature Patterns*

The definitions of the body-fixed reference frame $O_b(X_b, Y_b, Z_b)$, the camera centered attitude reference frame $O(X, Y, Z)$, and image coordinates (x, y), used in formulating the problem of attitude estimation based on a feature pattern, are shown in Fig. 8.2. The object feature pattern of an arbitrary shape is marked on the X_b-Y_b plane; and the moments of its images are used to estimate the three-dimensional object position and orientation.

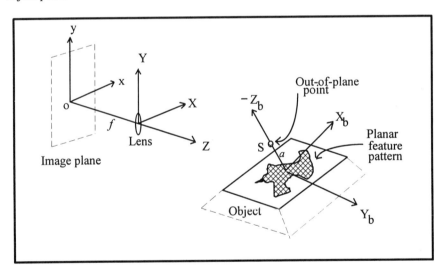

Fig. 8.2 Reference frames for 3D pose estimation using planar feature pattern.

We denote the initial and transformed image coordinates of the feature pattern by (x, y) and (x', y') respectively, the corresponding intensity functions by $f(x, y)$ and $g(x', y')$, and their geometric moments by m^f_{pq} and m^g_{pq}. Therefore,

$$m^f_{pq} = \int\int x^p y^q \ f(x, y) \ dx \ dy, \tag{8.4}$$

$$m^g_{pq} = \int \int (x')^p (y')^q \ g(x', y') \ dx' \ dy'. \qquad p, q = 0,1,2,3..... \qquad (8.5)$$

Assuming that the image intensity values are preserved during the transformation, we have

$$f(x, y) = g(x', y'). \qquad (8.6)$$

Further,

$$dx' \ dy' = \Delta \ dx \ dy, \qquad (8.7)$$

where Δ is the Jacobian of the transformation . Hence,

$$m^g_{00} = \Delta \ m^f_{00} . \qquad (8.8)$$

We use the following notations for the normalized first and second order moments of the initial and transformed images:

$$u_{pq} = m^f_{pq} / m^f_{00} ; \qquad v_{pq} = m^g_{pq} / m^g_{00} , \qquad p, q = 0,1,2,..... \qquad (8.9)$$

The above quantities are the moment features computed from the images required for the pose estimation algorithm. A general linear (affine) transformation of the object pattern in the three-dimensional space can be written in the following form:

$$\begin{bmatrix} X \\ Y \\ Z \end{bmatrix} = \begin{bmatrix} A_{11} & A_{12} & A_{13} \\ A_{21} & A_{22} & A_{23} \\ A_{31} & A_{32} & A_{33} \end{bmatrix} \begin{bmatrix} X_b \\ Y_b \\ 0 \end{bmatrix} + \begin{bmatrix} P \\ Q \\ R \end{bmatrix} \qquad (8.10)$$

The corresponding image transformation using a pin-hole camera model is

$$\begin{bmatrix} x' \\ y' \end{bmatrix} = \Lambda \begin{bmatrix} A_{11} & A_{12} \\ A_{21} & A_{22} \end{bmatrix} \begin{bmatrix} x \\ y \end{bmatrix} + \begin{bmatrix} P' \\ Q' \end{bmatrix} \qquad (8.11)$$

where Λ denotes the effective image scale factor of the transformed image with respect to the initial image (due to both projection and object translation), and P', Q' denote the relative shifts in the transformed image. If the initial image was taken at a distance R_0 (assumed to be known) from the object, and f is the focal length of the camera, then

$$\Lambda = R_0 / R ; \qquad P' = P f / R ; \qquad Q' = Q f / R \qquad (8.12)$$

The object pose-estimation problem essentially involves the determination of the unknowns A_{ij}, Λ, P', and Q'. The actual translational parameters of the object P, Q, R can then be obtained from Eq. (8.12). The expressions relating the image moments can be derived by substituting the image coordinate transformation (8.11), and different values of p and q, in Eq. (8.5). The moment equations up to second-order are given below.

$$m^g_{00} = \Lambda^2(A_{11}A_{22} - A_{21}A_{12})\, m^f_{00}$$

$$v_{10} = \Lambda\,(A_{11}\,u_{10} + A_{12}\,u_{01}) + P'$$

$$v_{01} = \Lambda\,(A_{21}\,u_{10} + A_{22}\,u_{01}) + Q'$$

$$v_{20} = \Lambda^2(\,A_{11}^2\,u_{20} + A_{12}^2\,u_{02} + 2A_{11}A_{12}\,u_{11}\,) + 2\,P'\,v_{10} - P'^2$$

$$v_{02} = \Lambda^2(\,A_{21}^2\,u_{20} + A_{22}^2\,u_{02} + 2A_{21}A_{22}\,u_{11}\,) + 2\,Q'\,v_{01} - Q'^2$$

$$v_{11} = \Lambda^2\{A_{11}A_{21}\,u_{20} + A_{12}A_{22}\,u_{02} + (A_{11}A_{22}+ A_{21}A_{12})u_{11}\,\} + P'v_{01} + Q'v_{10} - P'\,Q'$$

$$(8.13)$$

In order to reduce the amount of computation involved in solving the above set of equations, we first eliminate the unknowns Λ, P', Q'. After a series of algebraic manipulations on Eq. (8.13), we get the following matrix equation relating the initial and transformed image moments:

$$\frac{(A_{11}A_{22} - A_{21}A_{12})m^f_{00}}{m^g_{00}}\begin{bmatrix} v_{20} - v_{10}^2 \\ v_{02} - v_{01}^2 \\ v_{11} - v_{10}v_{01} \end{bmatrix} = \begin{bmatrix} A_{11}^2 & A_{12}^2 & 2A_{11}A_{12} \\ A_{21}^2 & A_{22}^2 & 2A_{21}A_{22} \\ A_{11}A_{21} & A_{12}A_{22} & A_{11}A_{22} + A_{21}A_{12} \end{bmatrix}\begin{bmatrix} u_{20} - u_{10}^2 \\ u_{02} - u_{01}^2 \\ u_{11} - u_{10}u_{01} \end{bmatrix}$$

$$(8.14)$$

The above equations are however not sufficient to determine all the pose parameters uniquely. We therefore consider the following third-order moment equation:

$$v_{30} = \Lambda\,(A_{11}^3\,u_{30} + A_{12}^3\,u_{03} + 3A_{11}^2 A_{12}\,u_{21} + 3A_{11}A_{12}^2\,u_{12}) +3P'v_{20} -3P'^2\,v_{10} + P'^3.$$
$$(8.15)$$

Substituting for P', Q' using equations in (8.13), we get

$$\Lambda^3 (K_1 - K_2) - \Lambda K_3 - K_4 = 0, \tag{8.16}$$

where

$$K_1 = A_{11}^3 u_{30} + A_{12}^3 u_{03} + 3A_{11}^2 A_{12} u_{21} + 3A_{11} A_{12}^2 u_{12},$$

$$K_2 = (A_{11} u_{10} + A_{12} u_{01})^3,$$

$$K_3 = 3 (A_{11} u_{10} + A_{12} u_{01}) (v_{20} - v_{10}^2),$$

$$K_4 = v_{30} + 2 v_{10}^3 - 3 v_{10} v_{20}.$$

The relative image scale factor Λ can now be eliminated from Eq. (8.13) and (8.16) to yield an equation in only the moment functions and the elements A_{ij} of the rotation matrix. This equation together with Eq. (8.14) can be considered as a system of four non-linear equation in the unknowns A_{11}, A_{12}, A_{21}, A_{22}, and solved using iterative numerical techniques like the Newton-Raphson's method. This set of equations significantly reduces the computational complexity, requiring only a 4x4 Jacobian matrix in the numerical solution. The remaining unknowns Λ, P', Q' can be got using the first three equations in (8.13) with the converged solution. The actual object translation parameters P, Q, R can then be obtained from Eq. (8.12).

The three-dimensional matrix $[A_{ij}]$ in Eq. (8.10) is orthonormal, for a rotational transformation. The 2x2 sub-matrix elements A_{11}, A_{12}, A_{21}, A_{22} therefore satisfy the equation

$$A_{11}^2 + A_{12}^2 + A_{21}^2 + A_{22}^2 = 1 + (A_{11} A_{22} - A_{21} A_{12})^2. \tag{8.17}$$

The above equation can be used as a constraint in the recursive algorithm to ensure proper convergence. It should also be noted that planar feature patterns always lead to rotational ambiguities, which are reflected in the mathematical formulation as a sign ambiguity in determining the attitude matrix elements A_{31}, A_{32}, A_{33}. In order to resolve this problem, it is necessary to use the additional image coordinate information of a point on the object located outside the plane of the feature pattern (point 'S' in Fig. 8.2). Closed-form solutions of the attitude parameters for the above problem can be found in [137].

8.2.2 Pose Estimation Using Invariant Feature Vectors

The shape characteristics of the images of general three-dimensional objects cannot be directly related to the three-dimensional object transformations, due to the presence of occluding surface elements. The algorithms considered in the previous section used a feature pattern which was completely visible throughout the allowable range of object motion, and provided a direct relationship between object and image transformations. In the absence of such a direct correspondence, image features obtained from several view directions can be stored as a reference library, and later compared with the features got for an unknown view of the object, to estimate the camera view angle direction. The algorithm presented in this section uses moment functions to construct invariant feature vectors for identifying the camera view angle, independent of the object distance and the orientation about the optical axis. The projection of a general three-dimensional rigid object onto an image plane, depends on the following parameters (Fig. 8.3).

(i) Camera view angle direction: α (azimuth angle), δ (elevation angle).
(ii) Camera orientation about the optical axis: σ.
(iii) Distance from the object : d .

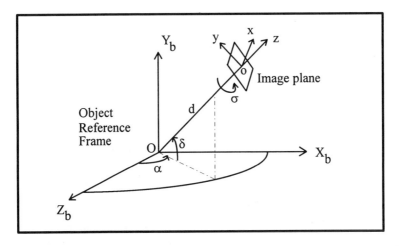

Fig. 8.3 Camera position and orientation parameters in the object reference frame.

The image plane coordinates (x, y) of an object point (X_b, Y_b, Z_b) are given by

$$x = \check{S}_f[\,(\cos \alpha \ \cos \sigma - \sin \alpha \sin \delta \sin \sigma)\, X_b + (\cos \delta \sin \sigma)\, Y_b$$
$$- (\sin \alpha \ \cos \sigma + \cos \alpha \sin \delta \sin \sigma)\, Z_b\,],$$

$$y = \check{S}_f[\,-(\cos \alpha \ \sin \sigma + \sin \alpha \sin \delta \cos \sigma)\, X_b + (\cos \delta \cos \sigma)\, Y_b$$
$$+ (\sin \alpha \ \sin \sigma - \cos \alpha \sin \delta \cos \sigma)\, Z_b\,],$$

$$(8.18)$$

where, $\check{S}_f$ denotes the image scale factor introduced by perspective projection.

The parameters σ, d denote the image transformations of rotation and scaling respectively. Any position offset of the camera optical axis also induces a translation of the image in its plane. Since the moment invariants of an image do not change with respect to the above transformations, they can be used to represent all images taken from a specific view angle direction (α, δ). A set of moment invariants can thus constitute a feature vector $V_{\alpha\delta}$ that represents the view angle direction. To this vector, we also append the zero order and second order central moments, for determining the attitude parameters.

$$V_{\alpha\delta} = \{\ \varphi_1,\ \varphi_2,\ \varphi_3,\ \varphi_4,\ m_{00},\ \mu_{20},\ \mu_{02},\ \mu_{11}\ \}. \tag{8.19}$$

In the above feature vector, the moment invariants φ will be used to identify the camera view angle direction α, δ ; the zero order moment m_{00} to obtain the camera distance d, and the second order central moments μ_{20}, μ_{02}, μ_{11} to obtain the camera orientation angle σ about the optical axis. The feature vectors $V_{\alpha\delta}$ are first computed for different known values of α, δ , and with fixed values of distance $d=d_0$, and angle $\sigma=0$, to generate a reference lookup table (Fig. 8.4). To include the representation of all possible views of the object in the reference library, we must have, $0 \le \alpha \le 2\pi$; $-\pi/2 \le \delta \le \pi/2$. In practice, the above range of values of α, δ is sampled in discrete steps (of say, 5 degrees) .

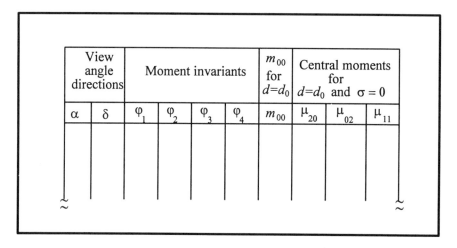

View angle directions		Moment invariants				m_{00} for $d=d_0$	Central moments for $d=d_0$ and $\sigma = 0$		
α	δ	φ_1	φ_2	φ_3	φ_4	m_{00}	μ_{20}	μ_{02}	μ_{11}

Fig. 8.4 Structure of reference lookup table for pose estimation using moment invariants.

Let

$$V' = \{ \varphi_1' , \varphi_2' , \varphi_3' , \varphi_4' , m_{00}' , \mu_{20}' , \mu_{02}' , \mu_{11}' \} \tag{8.20}$$

be the moment feature vector computed from an unknown arbitrary view of the object. The set of invariant moments $\{\varphi_1' , \varphi_2' , \varphi_3' , \varphi_4'\}$ is compared with the corresponding values in the reference library to determine the closest feature vector $V_{\alpha\delta}$ which matches with V'. The most common decision rule is the minimum Euclidean distance criterion, with appropriate weights added to each element to account for the large variation in the dynamic range of the moment invariants. Having obtained the values of α, δ, the third rotational parameter σ can be derived making use of the property that, when an image undergoes a rotation σ, the moment vector $(\mu_{20} - \mu_{02}, 2\mu_{11})$ rotates by an angle 2σ in the moment space [see Eq. (8.3)]. We can therefore write

$$\sigma = \frac{1}{2} \tan^{-1} \frac{2[\mu_{11}' (\mu_{20} - \mu_{02}) - \mu_{11}(\mu_{20}' - \mu_{02}')]}{(\mu_{20} - \mu_{02})(\mu_{20}' - \mu_{02}') - 4\mu_{11}\mu_{11}'} . \tag{8.21}$$

The distance d of the camera from the object along the view direction, is estimated as follows:

$$d = d_0 (m_{00} / m_{00}')^{1/2}. \tag{8.22}$$

The position of the origin of camera reference frame with respect to the body-fixed reference system can now be computed as

$$X_b = d \sin \alpha \cos \delta ,$$

$$Y_b = d \sin \delta ,$$

$$Z_b = d \cos \alpha \cos \delta . \tag{8.23}$$

8.2.3 *Attitude Estimation Using Moment Tensors*

In Chapter 6, we have seen that geometric moments can be viewed as contravariant tensors. The tensor properties can be effectively utilized to simplify the projection equations involving the object attitude parameters. Since the three-dimensional rotation of an object is always represented by an orthonormal matrix transformation, the corresponding three-dimensional moment tensors behave as absolute Cartesian tensors. If the object transformation is given by

$$y^i = a^i_j \, x^j \,, \tag{8.24}$$

then from Eq. (6.15), the moment tensor transformation is

$$\overline{T}^{ij\cdots} = a^i_k a^j_l \dots T^{kl\cdots} \,. \tag{8.25}$$

If s^{ij}, t^{ijk}, f^{ijkl}, v^{ijklm} denote the second, third, fourth, and fifth order central three-dimensional moment tensor components respectively, associated with the initial object orientation, then we can obtain three unit rank tensors t^k, f^k, v^k by simple contraction among the indices as follows:

$$t^k = t^{ijk} s^{ij} \,,$$

$$f^l = f^{ijkl} t^{ijk} \,,$$

$$v^m = v^{ijklm} f^{ijkl} \,. \tag{8.26}$$

Similarly, if $\bar{s}^{ij}, \bar{t}^{ijk}, \bar{f}^{ijkl}, \bar{v}^{ijklm}$ denote the second, third, fourth, and fifth order central moment tensors associated with the transformed object orientation, we can obtain the unit rank tensors $\bar{t}^k, \bar{f}^k, \bar{v}^k$. Using the transformation property of tensors in Eq. (8.25), we get the following linear equations in the unknowns a^i_j:

$$\bar{t}^j = a^i_j \, t^i \,,$$

$$\bar{f}^j = a^i_j \, f^i \,,$$

$$\bar{v}^j = a^i_j \, v^i \,. \tag{8.27}$$

From the above nine equations in nine unknowns, a solution to the rotation parameters a^i_j can be obtained.

8.3 Object Pose Estimation Using Stereo Images

The algorithms detailed in the previous sections used images obtained from a single camera to estimate the attitude and position parameters of an object. The problem of object pose estimation from monocular images generally leads to many singularity conditions and ambiguous solutions, which will have to be resolved by imposing appropriate constraints. A pair of images obtained simultaneously from two cameras in a stereoscopic configuration can be used to circumvent the problem of singular and ambiguous conditions occurring in object pose recovery from monocular images. Stereo images also contain redundant information which can be utilized to reduce the effects of image noise, thereby increasing the accuracy of the attitude and position estimates.

8.3.1 *Attitude Estimation Using Stereo Image Moments*

The information gathered from two images of a planar object, taken from different view directions, can be used to derive the three-dimensional orientation parameters uniquely. In this section, we consider a fixed configuration of two view directions, and the two-dimensional moments of the respective image intensity distributions, to derive a closed-form solution for the attitude elements without using any point correspondence information.

The definitions of the object and image reference frames used in the formulation of the problem of attitude estimation from multiple images, are shown in Fig. 8.5. The two image reference systems $o_1(x_1, y_1, z_1)$ and $o_2(x_2, y_2, z_2)$ are such that z_1, z_2 are along the respective view axes, the vectors $o_1x_1, o_1z_1, o_2x_2, o_2z_2$ are coplanar, (x_1, y_1) represents the image plane-1, and (x_2, y_2) represents the image plane-2. The initial orientation of the object plane coincides with the OXY plane. The two camera view angles make an equal angle λ with the Z-axis in the OXZ plane.

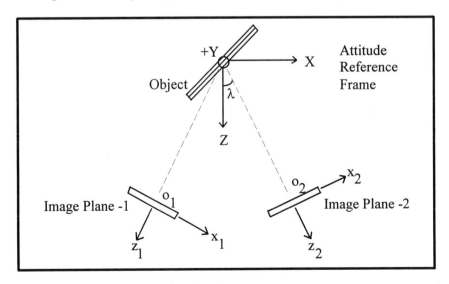

Fig. 8.5 Object and image reference frames for attitude estimation using stereo images.

If $A=[A_{ij}]$ denotes the three-dimensional attitude transformation matrix of the planar object, then the coordinate transformation relation is same as that given in Eq. (8.10), except that $P=Q=R=0$. The image coordinates in the two views are given by

$$\begin{bmatrix} x_1 \\ y_1 \end{bmatrix} = \check{S}_f \begin{bmatrix} \cos\lambda & 0 & \sin\lambda \\ 0 & 1 & 0 \end{bmatrix} \begin{bmatrix} X \\ Y \\ Z \end{bmatrix} \qquad (8.28)$$

$$\begin{bmatrix} x_2 \\ y_2 \end{bmatrix} = \check{S}_f \begin{bmatrix} \cos\lambda & 0 & -\sin\lambda \\ 0 & 1 & 0 \end{bmatrix} \begin{bmatrix} X \\ Y \\ Z \end{bmatrix} \qquad (8.29)$$

where $\check{S}_f$ is the unknown perspective projection scale factor of the image. Since we use only the initial and transformed images for attitude estimation, the projection scale factor does not appear in the following equations. The object space transformation given in Eq. (8.10) introduces corresponding image plane transformations as follows:

$$\begin{bmatrix} x_1' \\ y_1' \end{bmatrix} = \begin{bmatrix} C_{11} & C_{12} \\ C_{21} & C_{22} \end{bmatrix} \begin{bmatrix} x_1 \\ y_1 \end{bmatrix} \qquad (8.30)$$

$$\begin{bmatrix} x_2' \\ y_2' \end{bmatrix} = \begin{bmatrix} D_{11} & D_{12} \\ D_{21} & D_{22} \end{bmatrix} \begin{bmatrix} x_2 \\ y_2 \end{bmatrix} \qquad (8.31)$$

where

$$C_{11} = A_{11} + A_{31}\tan(\lambda); \; C_{12} = A_{12}\cos(\lambda) + A_{32}\sin(\lambda)$$

$$D_{11} = A_{11} - A_{31}\tan(\lambda); \; D_{12} = A_{12}\cos(\lambda) - A_{32}\sin(\lambda)$$

$$C_{21} = D_{21} = A_{21}\sec(\lambda); \quad C_{22} = D_{22} = A_{22} \qquad (8.32)$$

and (x_1', y_1'), (x_2', y_2') are the transformed coordinates of image-1, image-2 respectively. We denote the intensity functions of the initial image pair by $f(x_1, y_1)$,

$g(x_2, y_2)$; and the transformed image pair by $f'(x_1', y_1')$, $g'(x_2', y_2')$; and use the following notations to denote the moments of these functions:

m^f_{pq} = Two-dimensional moments of the initial image $f(x_1, y_1)$.

$m^{f'}_{pq}$ = Two-dimensional moments of the transformed image $f'(x_1', y_1')$.

m^g_{pq} = Two-dimensional moments of the initial image $g(x_2, y_2)$.

$m^{g'}_{pq}$ = Two-dimensional moments of the transformed image $g'(x_2', y_2')$.

$u_{pq} = m^f_{pq} / m^f_{00}$ [Normalized moments of initial image-1].

$u'_{pq} = m^{f'}_{pq} / m^f_{00}$ [Normalized moments of transformed image-1].

$v_{pq} = m^g_{pq} / m^g_{00}$ [Normalized moments of initial image-2].

$v'_{pq} = m^{g'}_{pq} / m^{g'}_{00}$ [Normalized moments of transformed image-2].

The object transformation in the three-dimensional space leads to the following moment equation on image plane-1 , due to the coordinate transformation given in Eq. (8.30):

$$m^{f'}_{pq} = \int_{x_1} \int_{y_1} (C_{11} x_1 + C_{12} y_1)^p (C_{21} x_1 + C_{22} y_1)^q \; f(x_1, y_1) \; \Delta \; dx_1 \, dy_1,$$

$$p, q = 0,1,2,3... \qquad\qquad (8.33)$$

where Δ is the determinant of the transformation matrix in Eq. (8.30). In the above equation, we have assumed that the intensity values are preserved during the transformation, so that $f'(x_1', y_1') = f(x_1, y_1)$.

Eq. (8.33) can be rewritten as

$$m^{f'}_{pq} = \Delta \int_{x_1} \int_{y_1} \{ \sum_{k=0}^{p+q} C_k \, x_1^k \, y_1^{p+q-k} \} \; f(x_1, y_1) \; dx_1 \, dy_1 \, ,$$

$$p, q = 0,1,2,3..... \qquad\qquad (8.34)$$

where C_k is the coefficient of $x_1^k \, y_1^{p+q-k}$ in the polynomial expansion of $(C_{11}x_1 + C_{12}y_1)^p (C_{21}x_1 + C_{22}y_1)^q$. Since, $m^{f'}_{00} = \Delta \, m^f_{00}$, from Eq. (8.34) we have

$$u'_{pq} = \sum_{k=0}^{p+q} \mathbf{C}_k \, u_{(k)(p+q-k)} \, , \qquad\qquad p, q = 0,1,2,3.... \qquad\qquad (8.35)$$

Similarly, the initial and transformed image moments on image plane-2 give

$$v'_{pq} = \sum_{k=0}^{p+q} \mathbf{D}_k \, v_{(k)(p+q-k)} \, , \qquad\qquad p, q = 0,1,2,3.... \qquad\qquad (8.36)$$

where $\mathbf{D}_k$ is the coefficient of $x_2^{\,k} \, y_2^{\,p+q-k}$ in the polynomial expansion of $(D_{11}x_2+D_{12}y_2)^p \, (D_{21}x_2+D_{22}y_2)^q$. Since the initial configuration of the planar object satisfies the equation $Z=0$, we have from Eq. (8.28) and Eq. (8.29), that

$$u_{pq} = v_{pq}, \quad \text{for all } p, q. \qquad\qquad\qquad (8.37)$$

By substituting different values for p, q in Eqs. (8.35), (8.36), the following moment equations can be obtained:

$$u'_{01} = C_{21} \, u_{10} + C_{22} \, u_{01}$$

$$u'_{02} = C_{21}^{\,2} \, u_{20} + 2C_{21}C_{22} \, u_{11} + C_{22}^{\,2} \, u_{02}$$

$$u'_{11} = C_{11}C_{21} \, u_{20} + (C_{11}C_{22} + C_{12}C_{21}) \, u_{11} + C_{12}C_{22} \, u_{02}$$

$$u'_{03} = C_{21}^{\,3} \, u_{30} + 3C_{21}^{\,2} C_{22} \, u_{21} + 3C_{21} \, C_{22}^{\,2} \, u_{12} + C_{22}^{\,3} \, u_{03}$$

$$u'_{12} = C_{11}C_{21}^{\,2} \, u_{30} + (C_{12}C_{21} + 2C_{11}C_{22}) \, C_{21} \, u_{21}$$

$$+ (C_{11}C_{22} + 2C_{12}C_{21}) \, C_{22} \, u_{12} + C_{12}C_{22}^{\,2} \, u_{03}$$

$$v'_{11} = D_{11}C_{21} \, u_{20} + (D_{11}C_{22} + D_{12}C_{21}) \, u_{11} + D_{12}C_{22} \, u_{02}$$

$$v'_{12} = D_{11}C_{21}^{\,2} \, u_{30} + (D_{12}C_{21} + 2D_{11}C_{22}) \, C_{21} \, u_{21}$$
$$+ (D_{11}C_{22} + 2D_{12}C_{21}) \, C_{22} \, u_{12} + D_{12}C_{22}^{\,2} \, u_{03}$$
$$(8.38)$$

The attitude estimation process is based on the solution of the system of equations (8.38) for the image transformation parameters C_{ij}, D_{ij} $(i, j = 1,2)$, from which the object transformation parameters A_{ij} can be computed. A block schematic of the attitude estimation procedure is given in Fig. 8.6.

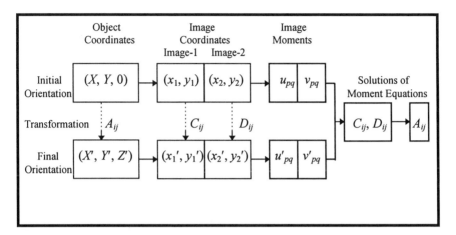

Fig. 8.6 Block schematic of attitude estimation procedure using stereo image moments.

Eliminating C_{21} from the first, second and fourth equations in (8.38), we get the following quadratic and cubic equations in C_{22} :

$$c_2 C_{22}^2 + c_1 C_{22} + c_0 = 0,$$

$$d_3 C_{22}^3 + d_2 C_{22}^2 + d_1 C_{22} + d_0 = 0, \tag{8.39}$$

where

$$c_0 = u'_{01}{}^2 u_{20} + u_{10}{}^2 u'_{02},$$

$$c_1 = 2 u'_{01}(u_{10} u_{11} - u_{01} u_{20}),$$

$$c_2 = u_{01}{}^2 u_{20} + u_{10}{}^2 u_{02} - 2 u_{01} u_{10} u_{11},$$

$$d_0 = u'_{01}{}^3 u_{30} + u_{10}{}^2 u'_{03},$$

$$d_1 = 3 u'_{01}{}^2 (u_{10} u_{21} - u_{01} u_{30}),$$

$$d_2 = 3 u'_{01}(u_{10}{}^2 u_{12} + u_{01}{}^2 u_{30} - 2 u_{01} u_{10} u_{21}),$$

$$d_3 = u_{10}{}^3 u_{03} - u_{01}{}^3 u_{30} - 3 u_{10}{}^2 u_{01} u_{12} + 3 u_{10} u_{01}{}^2 u_{21}. \tag{8.40}$$

From Eq. (8.39), we get

$$C_{22} = (d_2 c_0 c_2 - d_3 c_0 c_1 - d_0 c_2^2) / (d_3 c_1^2 - d_3 c_0 c_2 - d_2 c_1 c_2 + d_1 c_2^2). \tag{8.41}$$

The first equation in (8.38) can be rewritten as follows to give the value of C_{21} :

$$C_{21} = (u'_{01} - C_{22} u_{01}) / u_{10}. \tag{8.42}$$

The third and fifth equations in (8.38) can be treated as linear in the unknowns C_{11}, C_{12} and solved as

$$C_{11} = (u'_{11} e_1 - u'_{12} e_2) / (e_1 e_3 - e_2 e_4) \ ,$$

$$C_{12} = (u'_{12} e_3 - u'_{11} e_4) / (e_1 e_3 - e_2 e_4) \ , \tag{8.43}$$

where

$$e_1 \ = \ C_{21}^2 u_{21} + 2 C_{21} C_{22} u_{12} + C_{22}^2 u_{03}$$

$$e_2 \ = \ C_{21} u_{11} + C_{22} u_{02}$$

$$e_3 \ = \ C_{21} u_{20} + C_{22} u_{11}$$

$$e_4 \ = \ C_{21}^2 u_{30} + 2 C_{21} C_{22} u_{21} + C_{22}^2 u_{12} \ .$$

Similarly, the last two equations in (8.38) can be considered as linear in the unknowns D_{11}, D_{12} and solved as

$$D_{11} = (v'_{11} e_1 - v'_{12} e_2) / (e_1 e_3 - e_2 e_4),$$

$$D_{12} = (v'_{12} e_3 - v'_{11} e_4) / (e_1 e_3 - e_2 e_4). \tag{8.44}$$

The object's three-dimensional attitude transformation parameters A_{ij} can now be obtained from equations (8.32):

$$A_{11} = (C_{11} + D_{11}) / 2; \qquad\qquad A_{12} = (C_{12} + D_{12}) / (2 \cos(\lambda)) ,$$

$$A_{21} = C_{21} \cos(\lambda) ; \qquad\qquad A_{22} = C_{22} ,$$

$$A_{31} = (C_{11} - D_{11}) / (2 \tan(\lambda)); \quad A_{32} = (C_{12} - D_{12}) / (2 \sin(\lambda)). \tag{8.45}$$

Having thus obtained the elements of the first two columns of the matrix $\{A_{ij}\}$, the remaining elements of the matrix can be determined as follows, using the property that the column vectors of a rotational transformation matrix form an orthonormal triad [70]:

$$A_{13} = A_{21} A_{32} - A_{31} A_{22}$$

$$A_{23} = A_{31} A_{12} - A_{11} A_{32}$$

$$A_{33} = A_{11} A_{22} - A_{21} A_{12} \qquad (8.46)$$

8.3.2 *Position Estimation Using Stereo Image Moments*

We consider an *epipolar* camera geometry shown in Fig. 8.7, where two cameras of equal focal length f are arranged with their optical axes parallel and separated along the x-direction by a distance G. The camera coordinate reference systems $o_1(x_1, y_1, z_1)$ and $o_2(x_2, y_2, z_2)$ are parallel , with the image planes represented by the subsystems $o_1(x_1, y_1)$ and $o_2(x_2, y_2)$. The image intensity functions on these planes are denoted by $f_1(x_1, y_1)$ and $f_2(x_2, y_2)$. The three-dimensional object coordinate frame $O(X, Y, Z)$ has its origin fixed at the center of projection of the first camera, with axes directions parallel to the respective camera reference axes.

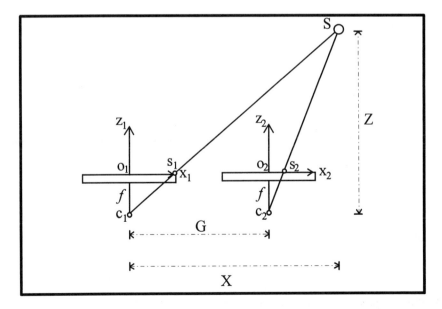

Fig. 8.7 Epipolar camera geometry.

The position coordinates (X, Y, Z) of an object point 'S' and its image points $s_1(x_1, y_1)$, $s_2(x_2, y_2)$ are related by the following expression:

$$\frac{Z}{f} = \frac{X}{x_1} = \frac{X-G}{x_2} = \frac{Y}{y_1} = \frac{Y}{y_2}. \tag{8.47}$$

The *pixel disparity* value at an image point (x_1, y_1) is denoted by $d(x_1, y_1)$, and restricted to the x-direction only. From Eq. (8.47), we have

$$d(x_1, y_1) = x_1 - x_2 = Gf/Z. \tag{8.48}$$

From the above equation, we see that the pixel disparity is inversely proportional to the depth of the imaged point.

If we assume that the intensity values are preserved at the corresponding pixels of both the images, then

$$f_1(x_1, y_1) = f_2(x_1 - d(x_1, y_1), y_1). \tag{8.49}$$

The object position coordinates in terms of the pixel coordinates and disparity value can be derived as

$$X = G x_1 / d(x_1, y_1); \qquad Y = G y_1 / d(x_1, y_1); \qquad Z = G f / d(x_1, y_1). \tag{8.50}$$

The method presented below uses one-dimensional image moments defined along corresponding rows of the stereo image pair to estimate the pixel-level disparity values. A *moment disparity function* is introduced as a similarity measure to establish the feature correspondence between a stereo image pair. The estimation of pixel disparity values is based on the minimization of the moment disparity function evaluated between row segments of the two images.

Consider an image row segment $\Re$ of length h pixels on the image plane $o_1(x_1, y_1)$ defined by

$$\Re = \{ f_1(x_1, y_1) : i_1 \leq x_1 \leq i_2, \quad y_1 \text{ fixed} \}, \tag{8.51}$$

where $i_2 - i_1 + 1 = h$.

A *disparity function* $d(x_1, y_1)$ can be thought of as a mapping from $\Re$ to a row segment $\Re'$ on the image plane $o_2(x_2, y_2)$ given by

$$\mathfrak{R}' = \{ f_2(x_1-d(x_1, y_1), y_1) : i_1 \le x_1 \le i_2, \quad y_1 \text{ fixed} \}. \tag{8.52}$$

We use the following definitions of one-dimensional moments of order p over image row segments $\mathfrak{R}, \mathfrak{R}'$. The summations are with respect to x_1 varying from 1 to h.

$$m_p(\mathfrak{R}) = \sum x_1^p \, f_1(x_1, y_1); \qquad m_p(\mathfrak{R}') = \sum x_1^p \, f_2(x_1-d(x_1, y_1), y_1),$$

$$n_p(\mathfrak{R}) = \sum (h+1-x_1)^p \, f_1(x_1, y_1); \quad n_p(\mathfrak{R}') = \sum (h+1-x_1)^p \, f_2(x_1-d(x_1, y_1), y_1)$$

$$\tag{8.53}$$

A vector, defined for each row segment, with moment functions evaluated over the pixel coordinates as components, is called a *moment vector* [e.g. $\{m_0, m_2, n_1, n_2\}$]. The components of the moment vector could be appropriately weighted to compensate for the range variations of the functions with respect to the order of the moments. If V is a moment vector on an image row segment $\mathfrak{R}$ of the first image, and V' the corresponding moment vector on a segment $\mathfrak{R}'$ of the same row of the second image, then the moment disparity function $D(\mathfrak{R}, \mathfrak{R}')$ is defined as the square of the Euclidean distance between the moment vectors. i.e.,

$$D(\mathfrak{R}, \mathfrak{R}') = |V - V'|^2. \tag{8.54}$$

The minimization of the moment disparity function is equivalent to the matching of the moment functions on $\mathfrak{R}, \mathfrak{R}'$ in a least-square sense, and can be used as a criterion for establishing region correspondence in stereo matching. Algorithms of this type, using one-dimensional image moments can be found in [157].

8.4 Conclusions

Image moments provide a convenient way to relate the object space transformations to the corresponding image shape variations, and therefore can be used to derive sufficient number of equations required for object pose recovery. Algorithms for estimating two-dimensional and three-dimensional object position and orientation parameters using the geometric moments of the initial and the transformed images, have been presented in this chapter. A feature vector based scheme using moment invariants to determine the pose of a general three-dimensional object, is also described. A method to determine the attitude parameters using moment tensors is also outlined.

Algorithms to estimate the orientation and position parameters from moment functions computed from stereo images have also been discussed. The application of moments in estimating the disparity levels in stereo images is also outlined.

References

- **2D Object Pose Recovery**: [7], [83], [88], [91], [92], [176], [215], [217].

- **3D Object Pose Recovery**: [10], [11], [12], [13], [22], [23], [44], [52], [70], [84], [123], [129], [130], [137], [138], [139], [141], [150], [203], [214].

- **Object Pose Estimation Using Stereo Images**: [140], [157].

Chapter 9
Miscellaneous Applications

The most frequent applications of moment functions are found in the areas of object recognition and pose estimation. Moments have also been used in several other applications such as edge detection and segmentation, image coding and reconstruction. Some of these application areas where significant results using image moments have been reported, are briefly described in this chapter.

9.1 Edge Detection

Image moments computed over small windows around each pixel have been used in detecting edges in the image [127]. An edge operator based on the moment-preserving principle using geometric moments computed over non-overlapping rectangular windows is detailed in Hsu [86]. A Zernike moment algorithm for sub-pixel edge detection given in [67] is briefly outlined below.

A *step edge* can be modeled as given in Fig. 9.1. An edge can be considered as a step change in the intensity value, say from h_1 by an amount k, to h_2. The sub-pixel level location and direction of the edge are specified by the distance l from the center of the pixel, and an angle ϕ from a reference x-direction.

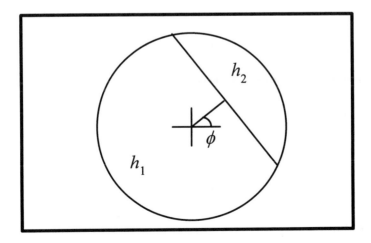

Fig. 9.1 Sub-pixel edge model.

If we rotate the edge by an angle $-\phi$, it will be aligned parallel to the y-axis, so that

$$\iint\limits_{x^2+y^2\leq 1} f'(x,y)\ y\ dx\ dy = 0 \tag{9.1}$$

where f'(x, y) is the intensity function after the rotation. If the Zernike moments of the original image and the rotated image are denoted by Z_{pq}, Z'_{pq} respectively, then from Eq. (5.24) we have

$$Z'_{00} = Z_{00}\ ; \qquad Z'_{11} = Z_{11}\ e^{i\phi}\ ; \qquad Z'_{20} = Z_{20}. \tag{9.2}$$

Since Eq. (9.1) is the imaginary part of Z'_{11}, we can write

$$\text{Im}[Z'_{11}] = \sin(\phi)\ \text{Re}[Z_{11}] + \cos(\phi)\ \text{Im}[Z_{11}] = 0 \tag{9.3}$$

where 'Re', 'Im' denote the Real and Imaginary components. Hence from Eq. (9.3) we get

$$\phi = -\ \tan^{-1}\!\left(\frac{\text{Im}[Z_{11}]}{\text{Re}[Z_{11}]}\right). \tag{9.4}$$

Thus Z_{11} can be obtained as

$$Z'_{11} = \cos(\phi)\ \text{Re}[Z_{11}] - \sin(\phi)\ \text{Im}[Z_{11}]. \tag{9.5}$$

Using the step edge model given in Fig. 9.1, we get [67]

$$Z'_{00} = h_1\pi + (k\pi/2) - k\sin^{-1}(l) - kl\,(1-l^2)^{\frac{1}{2}}$$

$$Z'_{11} = 2k\,(1-l^2)^{3/2}\,/\,3$$

$$Z'_{20} = 2kl\,(1-l^2)^{3/2}\,/\,3. \tag{9.6}$$

Solving the above equations for the unknown edge parameters, we have

$$l = Z_{20}\,/\,Z'_{11}$$

$$k = 3Z'_{11}\,/\,\{2(1-l^2)^{3/2}\}$$

$$h_1 = \{ Z_{00} - (k\pi/2) + k \sin^{-1}(l) + kl (1 - l^2)^{\frac{1}{2}} \} / \pi \tag{9.7}$$

Using Eq. (9.5), the above parameters can be computed from the Zernike moments Z_{00}, Z_{11}, and Z_{20}. The Zernike moments are evaluated over small neighborhoods around each pixel. Masks of size 5x5, for computing local Zernike moments at each pixel, are given in [67].

9.2 Texture Segmentation

The process of identifying regions with similar textures and separating regions with different textures is called *texture segmentation*. Texture segmentation is used in identifying surfaces and objects. A method for obtaining texture features directly from gray-level images by computing local moments is given in [202], and is briefly discussed below.

Texture features can be represented by local moments evaluated over small rectangular windows centered around each pixel in the image. The computation of local moments with 3x3 masks is described in Section 2.5.2. Images with larger texture tokens would require larger window sizes, whereas finer textures would require smaller windows. The set of values of a particular local moment function computed for all pixels in an image can be regarded as a *moment feature image*. For texture segmentation, a non-linear transducer is introduced which maps moment feature images to texture features. If $\{M_1, M_2, ... M_n\}$ denote a set of moment feature images obtained for n different local moment functions, then a texture feature image F_k corresponding to the moment image M_k with mean M_0 can be obtained as [202]

$$F_k(i,j) = \frac{1}{L^2} \sum_{(a,b) \in W_{ij}} |\tanh(\sigma(M_k(a,b) - M_0))| \tag{9.8}$$

where W_{ij} is an LxL averaging window centered at location (i, j); and σ is a constant, which controls the shape of the logistic function. Each pixel (i, j) thus has n texture feature values associated with it. The set of texture features at each pixel is denoted by a *texture feature vector* Ξ_{ij} defined by

$$\Xi_{ij} = < F_1(i,j), F_1(i,j), ... F_n(i,j) >. \tag{9.9}$$

The texture segmentation is done be applying a general purpose clustering algorithm to the texture features Ξ_{ij}.

9.3 Clustering and Thresholding

Clustering is the process of grouping pixels into different classes of intensity ranges. Classification of pixels into two groups (e.g., objects and background) is often used in bilevel thresholding to convert a gray image to a binary image. More generally, clustering can also be used to divide the whole range of gray values to several sub-ranges. This is called *multilevel thresholding*. A method for moment-preserving bi-level thresholding [200] is described below.

9.3.1 *Bi-level Thresholding*

Given an image with n pixels, and intensity distribution $f(x, y)$, the bi-level thresholding algorithm divides the intensity range into two classes, such that the intensity moments are preserved. The pth *intensity moment* of $f(x, y)$ is defined as

$$m_p = (1/n) \sum_x \sum_y \{f(x, y)\}^p, \qquad p = 0,1,2.... \qquad (9.10)$$

The above moments can also be computed from the histogram of the image as follows:

$$m_p = (1/n) \sum_k n_k \{g_k\}^p, \qquad p = 0,1,2.... \qquad (9.11)$$

where n_k is the total number of pixels with gray value g_k, in the histogram. Defining $c_k = n_k / n$, we get

$$m_p = \sum_k c_k \{g_k\}^p, \qquad p = 0,1,2.... \qquad (9.12)$$

If the image 'f' has to be replaced by a bi-level image with only two intensity values h_1 and h_2, with the number of pixels in each range being l_1, l_2 respectively; then the intensity moments of this image are

$$m_p' = \sum_{k=1}^{2} d_k \{h_k\}^p, \qquad p = 0,1,2.... \qquad (9.13)$$

where

$$d_k = l_k / n . \qquad (9.14)$$

d_k is the probability of a pixel in the image to have intensity value h_k. If the moments of the gray-level and the bi-level images are to be preserved, then

$$m_p' = m_p, \qquad\qquad p = 0,1,2.... \qquad\qquad (9.15)$$

From the above equations we get the following four equations in the four unknowns h_1, h_2, d_1, and d_2 :

$$d_1 + d_2 = 1$$

$$d_1 h_1 + d_2 h_2 = m_1$$

$$d_1 h_1^2 + d_2 h_2^2 = m_2$$

$$d_1 h_1^3 + d_2 h_2^3 = m_3. \qquad\qquad (9.16)$$

The solution for the unknowns from the above system of equations is given in [200]. The desired threshold value G can be chosen as the d_1-tile of the histogram as

$$d_1 = (1/n) \sum_{g_k \leq G} n_k . \qquad\qquad (9.17)$$

9.3.2 *Two-dimensional Clustering*

The bi-level thresholding process described above, identifies a point on the x-axis of the image histogram, and two intensity values on either side of it, by which the gray-level intensity range 'g' can be separated into two values h_1 and h_2. An extension of the bi-level thresholding is the two-dimensional clustering, where, a group of points in the two-dimensional plane has to be separated into two clusters by identifying a line of separation. A moment-preserving algorithm for two-dimensional clustering is given in [147], and is briefly outlined below.

The input pattern is represented by a set of complex numbers $\{z_i, i = 1,2,...N \}$, denoting the coordinates of the points. The origin of the coordinate system is shifted to the centroid of the pattern, so that the first order moment m_1 is zero. The second and third order moments are defined as

$$m_2 = \mathbf{E}[z z^*]; \qquad m_3 = \mathbf{E}[z z^* z] \qquad\qquad (9.18)$$

where z^* denotes the complex conjugate of z, and $E[]$ represents expectation. If the input pattern has to be replaced by two points h_1, h_2 (here h_1, h_2 are complex numbers) separated by a line of threshold, and if d_1, d_2 are the respective weights of these points [analogous to the probability defined in Eq. (9.14)], then the moment-preserving expressions are given by [see Eq. (9.16)]

$$d_1 h_1 + d_2 h_2 = 0$$

$$d_1 h_1 h_1^* + d_2 h_2 h_2^* = m_2$$

$$d_1 h_1 h_1^* h_1 + d_2 h_2 h_2^* h_2 = m_3. \qquad (9.19)$$

A generalized solution to the system of the above type is given in [147]. The line of threshold separating the input pattern into two classes is chosen as the perpendicular bisector of the line connecting the points h_1, h_2.

9.4 Image Reconstruction

This section discusses two image reconstruction methods using moment functions. The first one uses the property of orthogonal moments to reconstruct the intensity distribution using Fourier expansion theorem, and the second algorithm uses complex moments of a polygonal region to reconstruct the vertex points.

9.4.1 Image Reconstruction Using Orthogonal Moments

Images can be reconstructed from a sufficiently large number of orthogonal moments of the intensity distribution, using the respective inverse moment transforms. The equation for image reconstruction using Legendre moments is given in (4.13). Expressions for image reconstruction using Zernike moments are given in (5.20) and (5.21). While using the orthogonal moments of a binary image, the reconstructed intensity values will have to be appropriately thresholded. In the case of gray-level images, histogram equalization methods will have to be employed to further transform the intensity values to the valid range of a gray-levels. An illustrative example of the reconstruction of a binary shape of the letter 'E' using Legendre moments is given in Fig. 9.2. The maximum order of Legendre moments used in the reconstruction process is varied from 2 through 11, and the reconstructed image in each case, is shown in the figure above. The figure also shows the gross shape characteristics represented by low order moments, as well as more detailed and finer information content of higher order moments.

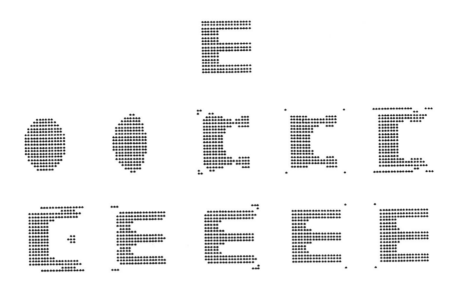

Fig. 9.2 The original image of the letter 'E', and the reconstructed images using Legendre moments.

9.4.2 *Polygon Reconstruction Using Complex Moments*

A method to reconstruct the vertices of a simply-connected planar polygonal region from a finite number of its complex moments is given by Milanfar [133]. The theorem underlying this method states that for any non-degenerate simply-connected n-gon P in the complex plane with vertices $z_j=x_j+iy_j$ $(j=1,2,...n)$, we have

$$k(k-1)\iint_P Z^{k-2} \, dx \, dy \; = \; \sum_{j=1}^{n} a_j z_j^k \, , \qquad \text{for all } k, \tag{9.20}$$

where

$$a_j \; = \; \frac{2A_j}{(z_j - z_{j+1})(z_j - z_{j-1})} \tag{9.21}$$

and A_j is the signed area of the triangle formed by the vertices z_{j-1}, z_j, and z_{j+1}. Defining the complex moments of the polygon P as

$$\tau_k = k(k-1)\iint_P Z^{k-2} \, dx \, dy \, , \tag{9.22}$$

the method given in [133] asserts that the vertices of the polygon P can be obtained from its moments as the roots of the polynomial

$$z^n + \sum_{j=1}^{n} p_j z^{n-j} = 0 \tag{9.23}$$

where the coefficients p_j are given by

$$\begin{bmatrix} p_n \\ p_{n-1} \\ \cdot \\ \cdot \\ \cdot \\ p_1 \end{bmatrix} = - \begin{bmatrix} \tau_0 & \tau_1 & \cdot & \cdot & \tau_{n-1} \\ \tau_1 & \tau_2 & \cdot & \cdot & \tau_n \\ \cdot & & \cdot & \cdot & \cdot \\ \cdot & & \cdot & \cdot & \cdot \\ \cdot & & \cdot & \cdot & \cdot \\ \tau_{n-1} & \tau_n & \cdot & \cdot & \tau_{2n-2} \end{bmatrix}^{-1} \begin{bmatrix} \tau_n \\ \tau_{n-1} \\ \cdot \\ \cdot \\ \cdot \\ \tau_{2n-1} \end{bmatrix}. \tag{9.24}$$

9.5 Moments and Transforms

This section gives the relationships between geometric moments and some of the popular transforms used in engineering applications. The expressions relating moments and transforms have been employed in several areas of image analysis. For example, the Fourier transforming property of a converging lens has been used for the optical computation of geometric moments [26],[197],[207]. The derivation of geometric moments from radon transforms have been used in the tomographic reconstruction of medical images [134].

9.5.1 *Fourier Transform*

The Fourier transform of the intensity function $f(x, y)$ in two dimensions is defined as

$$F(u, v) = \iint_\zeta e^{-2\pi i\,(ux+vy)}\; f(x, y)\; dx\, dy\,, \tag{9.25}$$

where $i = (-1)^{1/2}$, and (u, v) denote the spatial frequency coordinates. Re-writing the exponential term in series, and using the definition of geometric moments, one can derive

$$F(u, v) = \sum_{p=0}^{\infty} \sum_{q=0}^{\infty} \frac{i^{p+q}}{p!\,q!}\, u^p\, v^q\, m_{pq}\,. \tag{9.26}$$

From the above equation, it is easy to find that

$$\left[\frac{\partial^p \partial^q F(u,v)}{\partial u^p \partial v^q}\right]_{u=v=0} = i^{(p+q)}\, m_{pq}\,. \tag{9.27}$$

9.5.2 Hartley Transform

The Hartley transform of the function f(x, y) is defined as [208]

$$H(u, v) = \iint_{\zeta} f(x, y)\, [\cos\{2\pi\,(ux+vy)\} + \sin\{2\pi\,(ux+vy)\}]\; dx\, dy\,. \tag{9.28}$$

Analogous to the Fourier transform, we can derive the geometric moments from the Hartley transform of f(x, y) as follows:

$$\left[\frac{\partial^p \partial^q H(u,v)}{\partial u^p \partial v^q}\right]_{u=v=0} = \kappa(p,q)\, (2\pi)^{(p+q)}\, m_{pq}\,. \tag{9.29}$$

where

$$\kappa(p,q) = (-1)^{(p+q)/2}\,, \qquad \text{if} \quad p, q \text{ are even}$$

$$= (-1)^{(p+q-2)/2}\,, \qquad \text{if} \quad p, q \text{ are odd}$$

$$= (-1)^{(p+q-1)/2}\,, \qquad \text{otherwise.} \tag{9.30}$$

9.5.3 Hadamard Transform

The theoretical aspects related to the computation of geometric moments using the Hadamard transform, and its applications in the fast computation of moments are described in detail in [62]. A few of the important results given therein are outlined below.

The Hadamard transform $h(u,v)$ of $f(x,\ y)$ over the spatial coordinate space $1 \le x, y \le N$ is defined as

$$h(u,v) = \sum_{x=1}^{N}\sum_{y=1}^{N}(-1)^{\lambda(x,y,u,v)}.f(x,y) \tag{9.31}$$

where

$$\lambda(x,y,u,v) \equiv \sum_{i=0}^{n}u_i x_i + \sum_{i=0}^{n}v_i y_i \tag{9.32}$$

and $n = \log_2 (N)$. The symbols u_i, v_i, x_i, y_i stand for the ith bit of u, v, x, y respectively, and takes values 0 or 1. For example,

$$(u)_{\text{decimal}} = (u_n, u_{n-1}, \ldots u_1, u_0)_{\text{binary}} \tag{9.33}$$

The expressions relating the Hadamard transform $h(u,v)$ and the geometric moments m_{pq} of $f(x, y)$ are given below [62].

$$m_{00} = h(0,0)$$

$$m_{10} = \frac{N-1}{2}h(0,0) - \sum_{i=0}^{n-1}2^{i-1}h(0,2^i)$$

$$m_{01} = \frac{N-1}{2}h(0,0) - \sum_{i=0}^{n-1}2^{i-1}h(2^i,0)$$

$$m_{20} = \frac{(N-1)(N-2)}{6}m_{00} + (N-1)m_{10} + \frac{1}{2}\sum_{i=0}^{n-1}\sum_{j=0}^{n-1}2^{i+j}h(2^i+2^j,0)$$

$$m_{02} = \frac{(N-1)(N-2)}{6}m_{00} + (N-1)m_{10} + \frac{1}{2}\sum_{i=0}^{n-1}\sum_{j=0}^{n-1}2^{i+j}h(0,2^i+2^j)$$

$$m_{11} = \frac{-(N-1)(N-2)}{4}m_{00} + \frac{1}{2}(N-1)(m_{10}+m_{01}) + \frac{1}{4}\sum_{i=0}^{n-1}\sum_{j=0}^{n-1}2^{i+j}h(2^i,2^j).$$

$$\tag{9.34}$$

9.5.4 *Radon Transform*

The Radon transform $g(t,\theta)$ of a two-dimensional function $f(x, y)$ is defined as

$$g(t,\theta) = \iint \delta(x \cos\theta + y \sin\theta - t) \ f(x, y) \ dx \ dy \qquad (9.35)$$

The function $g(t,\theta)$ is defined for each pair (t,θ) as the integral of 'f' over a line L at an angle $\theta + \pi/2$ with the x-axis and at a radial distance t away from the origin (Fig. 9.3).

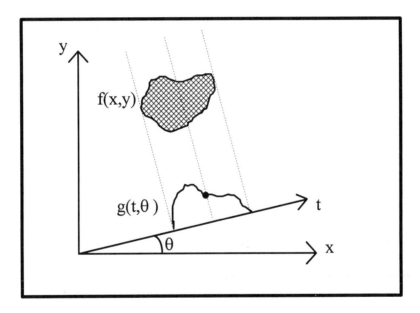

Fig. 9.3 Radon transform.

Consider the kth moment $g_k(\theta)$ of the function $g(t,\theta)$ as given below.

$$g_k(\theta) = \int t^k g(t,\theta) \ dt \qquad (9.36)$$

Using Eq.(9.35), we get the following relation in $g_k(\theta)$ and the geometric moments m_{pq} of the image $f(x, y)$:

$$g_k(\theta) = \sum_{j=0}^{k} \binom{k}{j} \cos^j \theta \, \sin^{k-j} \theta \, m_{j,k-j} . \tag{9.37}$$

9.6 Conclusions

Even though most of the application of image moments have been reported in the areas of object identification and positioning, several other interesting methods using moment functions have also appeared in literature. This chapter has introduced some of these methods. Algorithms for moment preserving edge detection, clustering and thresholding have been outlined. Local moments have been used as features for texture segmentation. Image reconstruction techniques using orthogonal and complex moments have been outlined. The relationships between geometric moments and various transforms used in engineering applications are also discussed.

References

- **Edge Detection**: [35], [38], [65], [66], [67], [86], [115], [122], [127], [165], [194].

- **Texture Segmentation**: [17], [104], [193], [204].

- **Clustering and Thresholding**: [106], [147], [200].

- **Image Reconstruction**: [36], [52], [100], [119], [125], [126], [132], [133], [134], [145], [196], [209].

- **Moments and Transforms**: [62], [82], [126], [134]., [207], [208].

Appendix 1
List of Moment Invariants

A list of geometric moment functions which are invariants with respect to image rotation, is given below. Additional properties like scale and translation invariance can be achieved by appropriate coordinate transformations and normalization described in Chapter 2.

1. $m_{20} + m_{02}$

2. $(m_{20} - m_{02})^2 + 4m_{11}^2$

3. $m_{20}\, m_{02} - m_{11}^2$

4. $(m_{30} - 3m_{12})^2 + (3m_{21} - m_{03})^2$

5. $(m_{30} + m_{12})^2 + (m_{21} + m_{03})^2$

6. $m_{30}^2\, m_{03}^2 - 6m_{30}\, m_{21}\, m_{12}\, m_{03} + 4\, m_{30}\, m_{12}^3 + 4\, m_{03}\, m_{21}^3 - 3m_{21}^2\, m_{12}^2$

7. $(m_{20} - m_{02})\, [(m_{30} + m_{12})^2 - (m_{21} + m_{03})^2] + 4\, m_{11}(m_{30} + m_{12})\, (m_{21} + m_{03})$

8. $(m_{30} - 3m_{12})\, (m_{30} + m_{12})\, [(m_{30} + m_{12})^2 - 3(m_{21} + m_{03})^2]$
   $+\ (m_{03} - 3m_{21})\, (m_{03} + m_{21})\, [(m_{03} + m_{21})^2 - 3(m_{12} + m_{30})^2]$

9. $(m_{03} - 3m_{21})\, (m_{30} + m_{12})\, [(m_{30} + m_{12})^2 - 3(m_{21} + m_{03})^2]$
   $-\ (m_{30} - 3m_{12})\, (m_{03} + m_{21})\, [(m_{03} + m_{21})^2 - 3(m_{12} + m_{30})^2]$

10. $(m_{30}\, m_{03} - m_{21}\, m_{12})^2 - 4(m_{03}\, m_{12} - m_{21}^2)\, (m_{30}\, m_{21} - m_{12}^2)$

11. $m_{40} + 2m_{22} + m_{04}$

12. $m_{40}\, m_{04} - 4m_{31}\, m_{13} + 3\, m_{22}^2$

13. $(m_{40} - m_{04})^2 + 4(m_{31} + m_{13})^2$

14. $(m_{40} - 6m_{22} + m_{04})^2 + 16(m_{31} - m_{13})^2$

15. $(m_{40} - 6m_{22} + m_{04}) [(m_{40} - m_{04})^2 - 4(m_{31} + m_{13})^2]$
$$+ 16(m_{40} - m_{04})(m_{31}{}^2 - m_{13}{}^2)$$

16. $(m_{31} - m_{13}) [(m_{40} - m_{04})^2 - 4(m_{31} + m_{13})^2]$
$$-(m_{40} - m_{04})(m_{31} + m_{13})(m_{40} - 6m_{22} + m_{04})$$

17. $m_{40}m_{22}m_{04} - 2m_{31}\, m_{22}m_{13} - m_{40}m_{13}{}^2 - m_{04}m_{31}{}^2 - m_{22}{}^3$

18. $(m_{50} + 2m_{32} + m_{14})^2 + (m_{05} + 2m_{23} + m_{41})^2$

19. $(m_{50} - 2m_{32} - 3m_{14})^2 + (m_{05} - 2m_{23} - 3m_{41})^2$

20. $(m_{50} - 10m_{32} + 5m_{14})^2 + (m_{05} - 10m_{23} + 5m_{41})^2$

21. $m_{60} + 3m_{42} + 3m_{24} + m_{06}$

22. $(m_{60} - 5m_{42} - 5m_{24} + m_{06})^2 + 16(m_{51} - m_{15})^2$

References

- **List of Moment Invariants**: [11], [13], [14], [57], [58], [85], [117], [118], [196], [203], [218].

Appendix 2
Moment Functions of a General Ellipse

Analytical expressions for computing the geometric and Zernike moments of a general ellipse are given below. The elliptical shape parameters used in these expressions are

a : Length of the semi-major axis.

b : Length of the semi-minor axis.

x_0, y_0 : Coordinates of the center of the ellipse.

λ : Angle which the major axis makes with the x-axis.

The following expressions are derived using the continuous integrals of the moment functions, assuming unit intensity value throughout the interior and boundary of the ellipse, and zero intensity value outside the ellipse.

Geometric Moments of the Ellipse

$$m_{00} = \pi\, a\, b$$

$$m_{10} = \pi\, a\, b\, x_0$$

$$m_{01} = \pi\, a\, b\, y_0$$

$$m_{20} = \pi\, a\, b \left(\frac{a^2 \cos^2 \lambda + b^2 \sin^2 \lambda}{4} + x_0^2 \right)$$

$$m_{02} = \pi\, a\, b \left(\frac{a^2 \sin^2 \lambda + b^2 \cos^2 \lambda}{4} + y_0^2 \right)$$

$$m_{11} = \pi\, a\, b \left(\frac{(a^2 - b^2)\cos \lambda\, \sin \lambda}{4} + x_0 y_0 \right)$$

$$m_{30} = \pi\, a\, b \left(\frac{3x_0 (a^2 \cos^2 \lambda + b^2 \sin^2 \lambda)}{4} + x_0^3 \right)$$

$$m_{03} = \pi\, a\, b \left(\frac{3y_0 (a^2 \sin^2 \lambda + b^2 \cos^2 \lambda)}{4} + y_0^3 \right)$$

$$m_{21} = \pi\, a\, b \left(\frac{y_0 (a^2 \cos^2 \lambda + b^2 \sin^2 \lambda)}{4} + \frac{x_0 (a^2 - b^2) \sin \lambda \cos \lambda}{2} + x_0^2 y \right)$$

$$m_{12} = \pi\, a\, b \left(\frac{x_0 (a^2 \sin^2 \lambda + b^2 \cos^2 \lambda)}{4} + \frac{y_0 (a^2 - b^2) \sin \lambda \cos \lambda}{2} + x_0 y^2 \right)$$

Zernike Moments of the Ellipse

$$Z_{00} = a\, b$$

$$Z_{11} = 2\, a\, b\, (x_0 - i\, y_0)$$

$$Z_{20} = 3\, a\, b \left(\frac{a^2 + b^2}{2} + x_0^2 + y_0^2 - 1 \right)$$

$$Z_{22} = 3\, a\, b \left(\frac{(a^2 - b^2)(\cos \lambda - i \sin \lambda)^2}{4} + (x_0 - i y_0)^2 \right)$$

Bibliography

1. Abu Mostafa Y.S, "Image normalisation by complex moments",IEEE Trans. on Patt. Anal. and Mach. Intell., Vol. 7, No. 1 (1985), pp. 46-55.

2. Abu Mostafa Y.S, "Recognitive aspects of moment invariants",IEEE Trans. on Patt. Anal. and Mach. Intell., Vol. 6, No. 6 (1984), pp. 698-706.

3. Alt F.L, "Digital pattern recognition by moments", Jnl. of the Assn. for Computing Machinery, Vol. 9, No. 2 (1962), pp. 240-258.

4. Anderson R.L, "Real time gray scale video processing using a moment generating chip", IEEE Trans. on Robotics and Automation, Vol. 1, No. 2 (1985), pp. 79-85.

5. Arbter K and Snyder W.E, "Application of the affine invariant Fourier descriptors to recognition of 3D objects", IEEE Trans. on Patt. Anal. and Mach. Intell., Vol. 12, (1990), pp. 640-647.

6. Arsenault H.H and Sheng Y, "Properties of the circular harmonic expansion for rotation invariant pattern recognition", Applied Optics, Vol. 25, (1986), pp. 3225-3229.

7. Awcock G.J and Thomas R (Eds.), Applied Image Processing (Macmillan : London : 1995), pp. 162-165.

8. Bailey R.R and Srinath M, "Orthogonal moment features for use with parametric and non-parametric classifiers", IEEE Trans. on Patt. Anal. and Mach. Intell., Vol. 18, No. 4 (1996), pp. 389-399.

9. Ballard D.H and Brown C.M (Eds.), Computer Vision (Prentice Hall : NJ: 1982), pp. 231-262.

10. Bamieh B.A and deFigueiredo R.J.P, "A framework and algorithms for identification and attitude determination of space objects from camera data", Rice University Tech. Report EE 8407, Houston (1984).

11. Bamieh B and deFigueiredo R.J.P, "Efficient new techniques for identification and 3D attitude determination of space objects from a single image", Intl. Conf on Robotics and Automation, (1985), pp. 67-71.

12. Bamieh B and deFigueiredo R.J.P, "General moment invariants and their application to 3D object recognition from a single image", Tech. Rep EE 8513, Dept of Elect and Comput Engg., Rice Univ., Houston TX , (1985).

13. Bamieh B and deFigueiredo R.J.P, "A general moment attributed graph method for three dimensional object recognition from a single image", IEEE Trans. on Robotics and Automation, Vol. 2, No. 1 (1986), pp. 31-41.

14. Belkasim S.O, "Pattern recognition with moment invariants -A comparitive study and new results", Pattern Recognition,Vol. 24, No. 12 (1991), pp. 1117-1138.

15. Belkasim S.O, "Shape-contour recognition using moment invariants", Intl. Conf. on Pattern Recognition, (1990), pp. 649-651.

16. Bhatia A.B and Wolf E, "On the circular polynomials of Zernike and related orthogonal sets", Proc. Cambridge Philos. Soc., Vol. 50, (1954), pp. 40-48.

17. Bigun J, "N-folded symmetries by complex moments in Gabor space and their application to unsupervised texture segmentation", IEEE Trans. on Patt.Anal.and Mach. Intell., Vol. 16, No. 1 (1994), pp. 80-87.

18. Bingcheng L, "The moment calculation of polyhedra", Pattern Recognition, Vol. 26, No. 8 (1993), pp. 1229-1233.

19. Born M and Wolf E (Eds.), Principles of Optics (Pergammon Press: NY : 1975), pp. 767-774.

20. Bougrenet J.L, "Scale-rotation invariant pattern recognition applied to image data compression", Pattern Recognition Lett., Vol. 8, No. 1 (1988), pp. 55-58.

21. Boyce J.F and Hossack W.J, "Moment invariants for pattern recognition", Pattern Recognition Lett., Vol. 1, No. 5 (1983), pp. 451-456.

22. Brochard J, "Modelling of rigid objects by bidimensional moments: Applications to the estimation of 3D rotations", Pattern Recognition, Vol. 29, No. 6 (1996), pp. 889-902.

23. Broida T.J and Chellappa R, "Estimating the kinematics and structure of rigid object from a sequence of monocular images", IEEE Trans. on Patt. Anal. and Mach. Intell., Vol. 13, No. 6 (1991), pp. 497-512.

24. Budrikis Z.L and Hatamian M, "Moment calculation by digital filters", AT&T Bell Lab Tech. Journal, Vol. 6, No. 2 (1984),pp. 217-229.

25. Casasent D, "Hybrid optical/digital moment based robotic pattern recognition system", Proc SPIE 360, (1982), pp. 105-111.

26. Casasent D and Cheatham L, "Optical system to compute intensity moments: Design", Applied Optics, Vol. 21, No. 19 (1982), pp. 3292-3298.

27. Casasent D and Cheatham L, "Image segmentation and real image tests for an optical moment based feature extractor", Optics Communications, Vol. 51, (1984), pp. 227-230.

28. Casasent D and Pauly J, "Infrared ship classification using a new moment pattern recognition concept", Proc SPIE 302, (1981), pp. 126-133.

29. Casasent D and Psaltis D, "Hybrid processor to compute invariant moments for pattern recognition", Optics Letters, Vol. 5, No. 9 (1980), pp. 395-397.

30. Casey R.G, "Moment normalisation of hand-printed characters", IBM J. Res Dev., Vol. 14, (1970), pp. 548-557.

31. Cash G.L and Hatamian M, "Optical character recognition by the method of moments", Comput. Vision Graphics and Image Process., Vol. 39, (1987), pp. 291-310.

32. Cheatham L, "Distortion invariant recognition using a moment feature space", Intl. Conf. on Comput Vision and Patt.Recgn, (1983), pp. 171-174.

33. Chen C.C, "Improved moment invariants for shape discrimination", Pattern Recognition, Vol. 26, No. 5 (1993), pp. 683-686.

34. Chen K, "Efficient parallel algorithms for the computation of two dimensional image moments", Pattern Recognition, Vol. 23, No. 1 (1990), pp. 109-119.

35. Chen L.H, "Moment preserving curve detection", IEEE Trans. Syst. Man and Cyber, Vol. 18, (1988), pp. 148-158.

36. Chen L.H, "Moment preserving sharpening: A new approach to digital picture deblurring", Comput. Vision Graphics and Image Process., Vol. 4, (1988), pp. 1-13.

37. Cheng S.C and Tsai W.H, "A neural network implementation of moment preserving technique and its application to thresholding", IEEE Trans. on Comput., Vol. 42, (1993), pp. 501-507.

38. Cheng S.C, "Image compression by moment-preserving edge detection", Pattern Recognition, Vol. 27, No. 11 (1994), pp. 1439-1449.

39. Cohignac T, "Integral and local affine invariant parameter and application to shape recognition", Intl. Conf. on Patt. Recgn. (1994), pp. 164-168.

40. Courant R and Hilbert D (Eds.), Methods of Mathematical Physics (Interscience :NY : 1953)

41. Cyganski D and Orr J.A, "A tensor operator method for identifying the affine transformations relating image pairs", Intnl. Conf. on Comput. Vision and Patt. Recgn., June 1993, pp. 361-363.

42. Cyganski D and Orr J.A, "Object identification and orientation in 3-space with no point correspondence information", Proc. Intnl. Conf. ASSP, (1984), pp. 23.8.1 - 23.8.4.

43. Cyganski D and Orr J.A, "Application of tensor theory to object recognition and orientation determination", IEEE Trans. on Patt.Anal.and Mach. Intell., Vol. 7, No. 6 (1985), pp. 662-673.

44. Cyganski D and Orr J.A, "Object recognition and orientation by tensor methods", in Advances in Computer Vision and Image Processing, T.S. Huang (Ed.), (JAI Press Inc. : 1988), pp. 101-144.

45. Dai M, "An efficient algorithm for the computation of shape moments from run length codes or chain codes", Pattern Recognition, Vol. 25, No. 10 (1992), pp. 1119-1128.

46. Davis P.J, "Plane regions determined by complex moments", Jnl. of approximation theory, Vol. 19, (1977), pp. 148-153.

47. Desai R and H.D.Cheng, "Pattern recognition by local radial moments", Intnl. Conf. on Patt. Recgn. (1994), pp. 168-172.

48. Dirilten H, "Pattern matching under affine transformations", IEEE Trans. on Computers, Vol. 26, No. 3 (1977), pp. 314-317.

49. Duda R.O and Hart P.E (Eds.), Pattern Classification and Scene Analysis (John Wiley : NY : 1973)

50. Dudani S.A, "Aircraft identification by moment invariants", IEEE Trans. on Computers, Vol. 26, No. 1 (1977), pp. 39-45.

51. Elliot E (Ed.), Algebra of Quantics (Oxford Univ Press : 1913).

52. Faber T.C, "Orientation of 3D structures in medical images", IEEE Trans. on Patt.Anal.and Mach. Intell., Vol. 10, No. 5 (1988), pp. 626-633.

53. Faugeral O.D (Ed.), Fundamentals of Computer Vision (Cambridge Univ Press : 1983).

54. Fausett L (Ed), Fundamentals of Neural Networks (Prentice-Hall : Englewood Cliffs : 1994).

55. Figueiredo R.J.P and Kehtarnavaz N, "Model based orientation independent 3D vision techniques", IEEE Trans. on Aerospace and Electronic Systems, Vol. 24, No. 5 (1988), pp. 597-607.

56. Flusser J, "Pattern recognition by affine moment invariants", Pattern Recognition, Vol. 26, No. 1 (1993), pp. 167-174.

57. Flusser J, "Affine moment invariants: A new tool for character recognition", Pattern Recognition Lett., Vol. 15, No. 4 (1994), pp. 433-436.

58. Flusser J, "Image features invariant with respect to blur", Pattern Recognition, Vol. 28, No. 11 (1995), pp. 1723-1732.

59. Flusser J and Suk T, "Recognition of blurred images by the method of moments", IEEE Trans. on Image Processing, Vol. 5, No. 3 (1996), pp. 533-538.

60. Freeman M.O, "Moment invariants in the space and frequency domains", Journal of Optical Soc. of America, Vol. 5, (1988), pp. 1073-1084.

61. Friedman J and Baskett F, "An algorithm for finding nearest neighbours", IEEE Trans. on Computers, Vol. 24, (1975), pp. 1000-1006.

62. Fu C.W, "Calculation of moment invariants via Hadamard transform", Pattern Recognition, Vol. 26, No. 2 (1993), pp. 287-294.

63. Galvez J.M and Canton M, "Normalization and shape recognition of three-dimensional objects by 3D moments", Pattern Recognition, Vol. 26, No. 5 (1993), pp. 667-681.

64. Ghorbel F, "A complete invariant description of gray-level images by the harmonic analysis approach", Pattern Recognition Lett., Vol. 15, No. 10 (1994), pp. 1043-1051.

65. Ghosal S, "Segmentation of Range images: An orthogonal moment based integrated approach", Intl. Conf on Robotics and Automation, Vol. 9, No. 4 (1993), pp. 385-399.

66. Ghosal S, "Zernike moment-based feature detectors", Intl. Conf. on Image Processing, (1994), pp. 934-938.

67. Ghosal S and Mehrotra R, "Orthogonal moment operators for subpixel edge detection", Pattern Recognition, Vol. 26, No. 2 (1993), pp. 295-306.

68. Gilmore J.F, "Building and bridge classification by invariant moments", Proc. SPIE - 292 (1981), pp. 256-263.

69. Gilmore J.F, "A survey of aircraft classification algorithms", Intl. Conf. on Pattern Recognition, (1984), pp. 559-562.

70. Golub G.H and VanLoan C.F (Eds.), Matrix Computations (Johns Hopkins Univ Press : MD : 1983).

71. Gonzalez R.C and Wintz P (Eds.), Digital Image Processing (Addison-Wesley : Mass : 1987), pp. 419-423.

72. Goodman J.W (Ed.), Introduction to Fourier Optics (McGraw-Hill : SanFrancisco : 1968).

73. Goshtasby A, "Template matching in rotated images", IEEE Trans. on Patt.Anal.and Mach. Intell., Vol. 7, No. 3 (1985), pp. 338-344.

74. Grace A.E and Spann M, "A comparison between Fourier-Mellin descriptors and moment based features for invariant object recognition using neural networks", Pattern Recognition Lett., Vol. 12, No. 10 (1991), pp. 635-643.

75. Gupta L and Srinath M, "Contour classification using invariant moments", IEEE Phoenix Conference on Comput & Commn., (1986), pp. 482-486.

76. Gupta L and Srinath M, "Contour sequence moments for the classification of closed planar shape", Pattern Recognition, Vol. 20, No. 3 (1987), pp. 267-272.

77. Gurevich G.B (Ed.), Foundations of the Theory of Algebraic Invariants (Noordhoff : Netherlands: 1964).

78. Hall E.L (Ed.), Computer Image Processing and Recognition (Academic Press: NY: 1979).

79. Hatamian M, "A real time two dimensional moment generating algorithm and its single chip implementation", IEEE Trans. on Accoust Speech and Signal Process, Vol. 34, No. 3 (1986), pp. 546-553.

80. He Z.Y and Wei G.Q, "A new algorithm for fast computation of moments of a binary image", Proc. IEEE Pacific Rim Conf. Commn. Comput. Signal Process., (1987), pp. 179-198.

81. Heywood M.I, "Fractional central moment method for moment-invariant object classification", IEE Proc. on Vision, Image and Signal Processing, Vol. 142, No. 4 (1995), pp. 213-219.

82. Hiriyannaiah H.P and K.R.Ramakrishnan, "Moments estimation in Radon space", Pattern Recognition Lett., Vol. 15, No. 3 (1994), pp. 227-234.

83. Horn B.K.P (Ed.), Robot Vision (McGraw-Hill : NY : 1986).

84. Horn B.K.P, "Closed form solutions of absolute orientation using unit quaternions", Jnl. of Optics Soc. of America - A, Vol. 4, No. 4 (1987), pp. 629-642.

85. Hsia T.C, "A note on invariant moments in image processing", IEEE Trans. on Syst Man and Cyber, Vol. 11, No. 12 (1981), pp. 831-834.

86. Hsu H.S, "Moment preserving edge detection and its application to image data compression", Optical Engineering, Vol. 32, No. 7 (1993), pp. 1596-1608.

87. Hsu Y.N, "Rotational invariant digital pattern recognition using circular harmonic expansion", Applied Optics, Vol. 21, (1982), pp. 4012-4015.

88. Hu M.K, "Visual pattern recognition by moment invariants", IRE Trans. on Infromation Theory, Vol. 8, No. 1 (1962), pp. 179-187.

89. Huang Z, "Affine invariant B-spline moments for curve matching", Intl. Conf. on Comput Vision and Patt.Recgn, (1994), pp. 490-495.

90. Hupkens.Th.M, "Noise and intensity invariant moments", Pattern Recognition Lett., Vol. 16, No. 4 (1995), pp. 371-376.

91. Hussain B, "Real time system for accurate three dimensional position determination and verification", IEEE Trans. on Robotics and Automation, Vol. 6, No. 1 (1990), pp. 31-43.

92. Jahne B (Ed.), Digital Image Processing (Springer Verlag: Heidelberg: 1971).

93. Jain A.K (Ed.), Fundamentals of Digital Image Processing (Prentice-Hall : NJ : 1989).

94. Jiang X.Y, "Simple and fast computation of moments", Pattern Recognition, Vol. 24, No. 8 (1991), pp. 801-806.

95. Kavianpour A, "Finding elliptical shapes in an image using a pyramid architecture", Computers and Electrical Engineering, Vol. 21, No. 1 (1995), pp. 69-75.

96. Khotanzad A, "Invariant image recognition by Zernike moments", IEEE Trans. on Patt.Anal.and Mach. Intell., Vol. 12, No. 5 (1990), pp. 489-497.

97. Khotanzad A, "Object recognition using a neural network and invariant zernike features", Intl. Conf. on Comput Vision and Patt.Recgn, (1989), pp. 200-207.

98. Khotanzad A, "Classification of invariant image representations using a neural network", IEEE Trans. on Accoust Speech and Signal Process, Vol. 38, No. 6 (1990), pp. 1028-1038.

99. Khotanzad A, "Rotation invariant pattern recognition using Zernike moments", Intl. Conf. on Pattern Recognition, (1988), pp. 326-328.

100. Khotanzad A and Hong Y.H, "Rotation invariant image recognition using features selected via a systematic method", Pattern Recognition, Vol. 23, No. 10 (1990), pp. 1089-1101.

101. Kim C.J and Shannon R.R, "Catalog of Zernike polynomials", In Applied Optics and Optical Engineering, (Ed) R.R. Shannon and J.C Wyant, Vol. 10 (Academic Press : SanDiego : 1987), pp. 193-221.

102. Kim W.Y, "A practical pattern recognition system for translation, scale and rotation invariance", Intl. Conf. on Comput Vision and Patt.Recgn, (1994), pp. 391-396.

103. Kintner E.C, "On the mathematical properties of the Zernike polynomials", Optica Acta, Vol. 23, No. 8 (1976), pp. 679-680.

104. Konepudy R, "Using moment invariants to analyse 3-D contour textures", Intl. Conf. on Image Processing, (1994), pp. 61-65.

105. Lee M, "Using moments to reduce object recognition to a one dimensional search", Intl. Conf. on Pattern Recognition, (1990), pp. 300-302.

106. Lee R, "Moment preserving detection of elliptical shapes in gray-scale images", Patt. Recgn. Lett., Vol. 11, (1990), pp. 405-414.

107. Lenz R, "A new method for unsupervised linear feature extraction using fourth order moments", Pattern Recognition Lett., Vol. 13, No. 12 (1992), pp. 827-836.

108. Leu J.G, "Computing a shape's moments from its boundary", Pattern Recognition, Vol. 24, No. 10 (1991), pp. 949-957.

109. Li B, "Range image based calculation of three dimensional convex object moments", Intl. Conf on Robotics and Automation, Vol. 9, No. 4 (1993), pp. 484-490.

110. Li B, "Two dimensional local moment, surface fitting and their fast computation", Pattern Recognition, Vol. 27, No. 6 (1994), pp. 785-790.

111. Li B.C, "Fast computation of moment invariants", Pattern Recognition, Vol. 24, No. 8 (1991), pp. 807-813.

112. Li B.C, "Pascal triangle transform approach to the calculation of 3D moments, Graphical Models and Image Process., Vol. 54, No. 4 (1992), pp. 301-307.

113. Li B.C, "A new computation of geometric moments", Pattern Recognition, Vol. 26, No. 1 (1993), pp. 109-113.

114. Li B.C, "Efficient computation of 3D moments", Intl. Conf. on Patt. Recgn. (1994), pp. 22-26.

115. Li B.C, "Moment difference method for the parameter estimation of a quadratic curve", Intl. Conf. on Patt. Recgn. (1994), pp. 169-172.

116. Li B.C, "High-order moment computation of gray-level images", IEEE Trans. on Image Processing, Vol. 4, No. 4 (1995), pp. 502-505.

117. Li Y, "Reforming the theory of invariant moments for pattern recognition", Pattern Recognition, Vol. 25, No. 7 (1992), pp. 723-730.

118. Li Y, "Fourier-Mellin transform and the invariant image moments", Japn. Journal of Applied Physics, Vol. 30, (1991), pp. 1405-1406.

119. Liao S.X and Pawlak M, "On image analysis by moments", IEEE Trans. on Patt. Anal. and Mach. Intell., Vol. 18, No. 3 (1996), pp. 254-266.

120. Lin F and Brandt R.D, "Towards absolute invariants of images under translation, rotation and dilation", Pattern Recognition Lett., Vol. 14, No. 5 (1993), pp. 369-379.

121. Lippman R.P, "An introduction to computing with neural nets", IEEE ASSP Magazine, Vol. 4, (Apr 1987), pp. 4-22.

122. Liu S.T and Tsai W.H, "Moment preserving curve detection", Pattern Recognition, Vol. 23, (1990), pp. 441-460.

123. Lo C.H, "Pattern recognition using 3D moments", Intl. Conf. on Pattern Recognition, (1990), pp. 540-544.

124. Lo C.H and Don H.S, "3D moment forms. Their construction and application to object identification and positioning", IEEE Trans. on Patt.Anal.and Mach. Intell., Vol. 11, No. 10 (1989), pp. 1053-1064.

125. Lucas D, "Techniques to exploit relation between polynominal representation and moments of pictures", Intl. Conf. on Comput Vision and Patt.Recgn, (1985), pp. 138-143.

126. Lucas D, "Moment techniques in picture analysis", Intl. Conf. on Comput Vision and Patt.Recgn, (1983), pp. 178-187.

127. Lyvers E.P, "Subpixel measurements using a moment-based edge operator", IEEE Trans. on Patt.Anal.and Mach. Intell., Vol. 11, No. 12 (1989), pp. 1293-1308.

128. Maitra S, "Moment invariants", IEEE Proceedings, Vol. 67, No. 4 (1979), pp. 697-699.

129. Markandey V and Figueiredo R.J.P, "Robot sensing techniques based on high dimensional moment invariants and tensors", IEEE Trans. on Robotics and Automation, Vol. 8, No. 2 (1992), pp. 186-195.

130. Markandey V and deFigueiredo, "A technique for 3D Robot vision for space applications", Proc. of the JPL space telerobotics workshop, Jan 1987.

131. Mertzios B.G and Tsirikolias K, "Fast shape descrimination via one dimensional moments", Intl. Conf. on Accoust. Speech and Signal Process., (May 1991), pp. 2473-2475.

132. Milanfar P, "Moment based geometric image reconstruction", Intl. Conf. on Image Processing, (1994), pp. 825-829.

133. Milanfar P, "Reconstructing polygons from moments with connections to array processing", MIT Report, CICS-P-389, (1994).

134. Milanfar P, "A moment-based variational approach to tomographic reconstruction", IEEE Trans. on Image Processing, Vol. 5, No. 3 (1996), pp. 459-470.

135. Mingfa Z, "Pattern recognition with moment invariants on a machine vision system", Pattern Recognition Lett., Vol. 9, No. 3 (1989), pp. 175-180.

136. Mukundan R, "A numerical approximation of two dimensional image moments", Indian Journal of Pure and Applied Mathematics, Vol. 22, No. 10 (1991), pp. 879-886.

137. Mukundan R, "Estimation of quaternion parameters from two dimensional image moments", Graphical Models and Image Processing -CVGIP, Vol. 54, No. 4 (1992), pp. 345-350.

138. Mukundan R, "Attitude estimation using moment invariants", Pattern Recognition Lett., Vol. 14, No. 3 (1993), pp. 199-205.

139. Mukundan R, "Image based attitude and position estimation using moment functions". Ph.D dissertation (Indian Institute of Science: July 1995).

140. Mukundan R, N.K. Malik, K.R. Ramakrishnan, "Estimation of object orientation from a pair of images using moment functions", Proceedings of Intnl. Sysmposium on Intelligent Robotics, (ISIR-93, Jan 1993), pp. 866-875.

141. Mukundan R, K.R.Ramakrishnan,"Fast computation of Legendre and Zernike moments", Pattern recognition, Vol. 28, No. 9, (Sep 1995), pp. 1433-1442.

142. Ngan K.N, "Fuzzy quaternion approach to object recognition incorporating Zernike moment invariants", Intl. Conf. on Pattern Recognition, (1990), pp. 288-290.

143. Pan F and Keane M, "A new set of moment invariants for handwritten numeral recognition", Intl. Conf. on Image Processing, (1994), pp. 154-158.

144. Pan Y, "A note on efficient parallel algorithms for the computation of two dimensional image moments", Pattern Recognition, Vol. 24, No. 9 (1991), pp. 917-917.

145. Papademetriou R.C, "Reconstructing with moments", Proc. 11th IAPR Intnl. Conf. on Patt. Recgn., Vol. 3 (1992), pp. 476-480.

146. Pawlak M, "On the reconstruction aspects of moment descriptors", IEEE Trans. on Information Theory, Vol. 38, No. 6 (1992), pp. 1698-1708.

147. Pei S.C and Cheng C.M, "A fast two-class classifier for 2D data using complex moment preserving principle", Pattern Recognition, Vol. 29, No. 3 (1996), pp. 519-531.

148. Perantonis S and Lisboa P, "Translation, rotation and scale invariant pattern recognition by high order neural networks and moment classifiers", IEEE Trans. on Neural Networks, Vol. 3, (1992), pp. 241-251.

149. Philips W, "A new fast algorithm for moment computation", Pattern Recognition, Vol. 26, No. 11 (1993), pp. 1619-1621.

150. Pinjo Z and Cyganski D, "Determination of 3D object orientations from projections", Pattern Recognition Lett., Vol. 3, No. 5 (1985), pp. 351-356.

151. Ponlo R.J, "New invariants for three dimensional recognition", Intl. Conf on Comput Vision Represenation and Contrl , (1984), pp. 158-162.

152. Poularikas A.D (Ed), The Transforms and Applications (CRC Press: Florida : 1996).

153. Prada A and Rusch W, "Algorithm for computation of Zernike polynomial expansion coefficients", Applied Optics, Vol. 28 , (1989), pp. 749-754.

154. Pratt W.K (Ed.), Digital Image Processing (John Wiley : NY : 1978).

155. Prokop R.J and Reeves A.P, "A survey of moment based techniques for unoccluded object representation", Graphical Models and Image Processing -CVGIP, Vol. 54, No. 5 (1992), pp. 438-460.

156. Pun T and Eden M, "Estimation of first and second order moments of a quantised signal", Signal Processing, Vol. 10, No. 2 (1986), pp. 115-127.

157. Ramakrishnan K.R, R. Mukundan, "Estimation of stereo disparity using moment functions", The third intnl. Conf. on Automation, Robotics and Comput. Vision (ICARCV-94) , Vol. 1, WA2.3, (Nov 1994), pp. 30-34.

158. Ranganathan N, "An efficient VLSI architecture for template matching based on moment preserving pattern matching", Intnl. Conf. on Patt. Recgn., (1994), pp. 388-390.

159. Raveendran P and Omatu S, "Performance of an optimal subset of Zernike features for pattern classification", Information Sciences, Vol. 1, (1993), pp. 133-147.

160. Reddi S.S, "Radial and angular moment invariants for image identification", IEEE Trans. on Patt. Anal. and Mach. Intell., Vol. 3, No. 2 (1981), pp. 240-242.

161. Reeves A.P, "Shape analysis of segmental objects using moments", Intl. Conf. on Pattern Recognition, (1981), pp. 171-176.

162. Reeves A.P, "The general theory of moments for shape analysis and the parallel implementation of moment operations", Purdue Univ. Tech. Report No. TR-EE 81-37, (Oct 1981).

163. Reeves A.P, "A parallel mesh moment computer", Intl. Conf. on Pattern Recognition, (1982), pp. 465-467.

164. Reeves A.P, "Shape analysis of three dimensional objects using the method of moments", Intl. Conf. on Comput Vision and Patt.Recgn, (1983), pp. 20-26.

165. Reeves A.P, "A moment based two-dimensional edge operator", Proc. IEEE Conf on Comput Vision and Pattern Recogn., (1983), pp. 312-317.

166. Reeves A.P, "Three dimensional shape analysis using moments and fourier descriptors", IEEE Trans. on Patt. Anal. and Mach. Intell., Vol. 10, No. 6 (1988), pp. 937-942.

167. Reeves A.P, "Identification of three dimensional objects using range information", IEEE Trans. on Patt. Anal.and Mach. Intell., Vol. 11, No. 4 (1989), pp. 403-410.

168. Reiss T.H, "The revised fundamental theorem of moment invariants", IEEE Trans. on Patt. Anal.and Mach. Intell., Vol. 13, No. 8 (1991), pp. 830-834.

169. Rosenfeld A and Kak A.C (Eds.), Digital Picture Processing, Second Edn., Vol. 2 (Academic Press: Orlando: 1982).

170. Rothe I, "The method of normalization to determine invariants", IEEE Trans. on Patt. Anal. and Mach. Intell., Vol. 18, No. 4 (1996), pp. 366-376.

171. Rumelhart D.E and McClelland J.L, "Parallel distributed processing; Explorations in the micro structure of cognition" Vol. 1 - Foundations, (MIT Press : Cambridge : 1986).

172. Sadjadi F.A, "Three dimensional moment invariants", IEEE Trans. on Patt. Anal.and Mach. Intell., Vol. 2, No. 2 (1980), pp. 127-136.

173. Sadjadi F.A, "Numerical computation of moment invariants", Intl. Workshop on Patt.Recgn and Image Process, (1978), pp. 181-187.

174. Sadjadi F.A and Hall E.L, "Object recognition using three dimensional moment invariants", Intl. Conf. on Pattern Recognition, (1979), pp. 327-332.

175. Safaee-Rad R, "Application of moment and Fourier descriptors to the accurate estimation of elliptical shape parameters", Pattern Recognition Lett., Vol. 13, No. 7 (1992), pp. 497-508.

176. Salzman D, "A method of general moments for orienting 2D projections of unknown 3D objects", Comput. Vision Graphics and Image Process., Vol. 50, (1990), pp. 129-156.

177. Sansone G (Ed.), Orthogonal Functions (Interscience : NY : 1955).

178. Sardana H.K, "Global description of edge patterns using moments", Pattern Recognition, Vol. 27, No. 1 (1994), pp. 109-118.

179. Sardana H.K, "Edge moment based three dimensional object recognition", Optical Engineering, Vol. 33, No. 10 (1994), pp. 3398-3405.

180. Sheng Y, "Experiments on pattern recognition using invariant Fourier-Mellin desriptors", Journal of the Optical Society of America, Vol. 3, No. 6 (1986), pp. 771-776.

181. Sheng Y, "Circular Fourier Radial Mellin transform descriptors for pattern recognition", Journal of the Optical Society of America, Vol. 3, No. 6 (1986), pp. 885-888.

182. Sheng Y, "Orthogonal Fourier-Mellin moments for invariant pattern recognition", Journal of the Optical Society of America, Vol. 11, No. 6 (1994), pp. 1748-1757.

183. Singer M.H, "A general approach to moment calculation for polygons and line segments", Pattern Recognition, Vol. 26, No. 7 (1993), pp. 1019-1028.

184. Siu W.C, "Efficient computation of moments for pattern recognition", IEEE Pacific Rim Conf. on Comm., Comput., Sig Proc., Vicotria (1991), pp. 589-592.

185. Siu W.C, "Fast realization of two-dimensional image moments", Proc. IEEE Workshop on visual signal processing and commn., (1991), pp. 6-7.

186. Siu W.C et. al., "An analysis on the realisation of two dimensional image moments", Proc. IEEE Intnl. Symposium on Circuits and Systems (1992), pp. 726-729.

187. Sluzek A, "Using moment invariants to recognize and locate partially occluded 2D objects", Pattern Recognition Lett.,Vol. 7, No. 4 (1988), pp. 253-257.

188. Sluzek A, "Identification of planar objects in 3D space from perspective projections", Pattern Recognition Lett., Vol. 7, No. 1 (1988), pp. 59-63.

189. Sluzek A, "Identification and inspection of 2D objects using new moment-based shape descriptors", Pattern Recognition Lett., Vol. 16, No. 7 (1995), pp. 687-697.

190. Smith F.W and Wright M.H, "Automatic ship photo interpretation by the method of moments", IEEE Trans. on Computers, Vol. 20, No. 9 (1971), pp. 1089-1095.

191. Strachan N.J.C, "A method for working out the moments of a polygon using an integration technique", Pattern Recognition Lett., Vol. 11, No. 5 (1990), pp. 351-354.

192. Sugisaka M, "Fast pattern recognition by using moment invariants computation via artificial neural networks", Control Theory and Advanced Technology, Vol. 9, No. 4, 1993, pp. 877-886.

193. Super B.J, "Shape from texture using local spectral moments", IEEE Trans. on Patt. Anal. and Mach. Intell., Vol. 17, No. 4 (1995), pp. 333-343.

194. Tabatabai A.J and Mitchell R, "Edge location to sub-pixel values in digital imagery", IEEE Trans. on Patt. Anal. and Mach. Intell., Vol. 6, No. 2 (1984), pp. 188-201.

195. Taubin G and Cooper D.B, "Object recognition based on moment invariants", in Geometric Invariance in Computer Vision , Mundy J.L and Zisserman A (Eds.), (MIT Press: Mass: 1992), pp. 375-397.

196. Teague M.R, "Image analyis via the general theory of moments", Journal of the Optical Society of America, Vol. 70, No. 8 (1980), pp. 920-930.

197. Teague M.R, "Optical calculation of image moments", Applied Optics, Vol. 19, No. 8 (1980), pp. 1353-1356.

198. Teh C.H, "On digital approximation of moment invariants", Computer Vision Graphics and Image Processing, Vol. 33, No. 3 (1986), pp. 318-326.

199. Teh C.H and Chin R.T, "On image analysis by the method of moments", IEEE Trans. on Patt.Anal.and Mach. Intell., Vol. 10, No. 4 (1988), pp. 496-513.

200. Tsai W.H, "Moment preserving thresholding - A new approach", Comput. Vision Graphics and Image Process., Vol. 29, No. 3 (1985), pp. 377-393.

201. Tsirikolias K, "Statistical pattern recognition using efficient two dimensional moments with applications", Pattern Recognition, Vol. 26, No. 6 (1993), pp. 877-882.

202. Tuceryan M, "Moment based texture segmentation", Pattern Recognition Lett., Vol. 15, No. 7 (1994), pp. 659-667.

203. Tzafestas S, "A numeric symbolic expert system for 2D and 3D object recognition in robotic applications", Mathematics and Computers for Simulation, Vol. 32, No. 4 (1990), pp. 403-418.

204. Tzannes N.S, "Maximum entropy reconstruction of moment coded images", Optical Engineering, Vol. 26, No. 10 (1987), pp. 1077-1083.

205. Ullman J.R (Ed.), Pattern Recognition Techniques (Butterworths : London : 1973).

206. Vernon D, "Two dimensional object recognition using partial contours", Image and Vision Computing, Vol. 5, No. 1 (1987), pp. 21-27.

207. Vijayakumar B.V.K, "Calculation of geometric moments using Fourier plane intensities", Applied Optics, Vol. 25, No. 6 (1986), pp. 997-1007.

208. Vijayakumar B.V.K, "Geometric moments computed from the Hartley Transform", Optical Engineering, Vol. 25, No. 12 (1986), pp. 1327-1356.

209. Wallin A, "Complete sets of complex zernike moment invariants and the role of pseudo invariants", IEEE Trans. on Patt. Anal. and Mach. Intell., Vol. 17, No. 11 (1995), pp. 1106-1110.

210. Wang S.S, "Invariant pattern recognition by moment fourier descriptor", Pattern Recognition, Vol. 27, No. 12 (1994), pp. 1735-1742.

211. Wechsler H, "Invariance in pattern recognition", in Advances in Electronics and Electron Physics, Hawkes P.W (Ed.), Vol. 69 (1987), pp. 261-322.

212. Weiss I, "Geometric invariants and object recognition", Intnl. J. of Computer Vision, Vol. 10 (1993), pp. 207-231.

213. Wiejak J.S, "Moment invariants in theory and practice", Image and Vision Computing, Vol. 1, No. 2 (1983), pp. 79-83.

214. Wlczek P et.al., "Pose estimation of three-dimensional objects from single camera images", Digital Signal Processing, Vol. 5, (1985), pp. 176-183.

215. Wohn K, "Estimating the finite displacement using moments", Pattern Recognition Lett., Vol. 11, No. 5 (1990), pp. 371-378.

216. Wong R.Y and Hall E.L, "Scene matching with invariant moments", Computer Vision Graphics and Image Processing, Vol. 8, No. 1 (1978), pp. 16-24.

217. Wong R.Y and Hall E.L, "Image transformations", Intl. Conf. on Pattern Recognition, (1978), pp. 939-942.

218. Wong W.H, "Generation of moment invariants and their uses for character recognition", Pattern Recognition Lett., Vol. 16, No. 2 (1995), pp. 115-123.

219. Wood J, "Invariant pattern recognition : A review", Pattern Recognition, Vol. 29, No. 1 (1996), pp. 1-17.

220. Xu X, "Practical issues concerning moment invariants", Jnl. of Systems Engineering and Electronics, Vol. 7, No. 1 (1996), pp. 43-57.

221. Yang L, "Fast computation of invariant geometric moments: A new method giving correct results", Intl. Conf. on Patt. Recgn. (1994), pp. 201-204.

222. Yang L, "Fast and exact computation of cartesian geometric moments using discrete Green's theorem", Pattern Recognition, Vol. 29, No. 7 (1996), pp. 1061-1073.

223. You S.D, Ford G.E, "Network model for invariant object recognition", Pattern Recognition Lett., Vol. 15, No. 7 (1994), pp. 761-767.

224. Zakaria M.F, "Fast algorithm for the computation of moment invariants", Pattern Recognition, Vol. 20, No. 6 (1987), p 639-643.

225. Zernike F (Ed.), Physica, Vol. 1, (1934), pp. 689-704 (in German).

226. Zusne L, "Moments of area and of the perimeter of visual form as predictors of discrimination performance", Jnl. of Experimental Psychology, Vol. 69 (1965), pp. 213-220.

Index

A

Absolute tensor 72
Affine transformations 15, 72, 96
Algebraic form 20
Algebraic invariants 20
Alternation of tensors 73
Aspect ratio invariants 18
Auto-correlation function 32

B

Back-propagation algorithm 90
Basis set 2
Bi-level thresholding 116
Blur invariants 24
Boundary moments 11

C

Cartesian moments 9
Cayley's notation 20
Central moments 12, 36
Centroid of image 12, 35
Characteristic function 10
Circular harmonic transform 42
Clustering 116
Complex moments 39, 45
Contour integration 28, 67
Contraction of tensors 73
Contragradient vectors 21
Contrast invariants 24
Contravariant index 72
Correlation coefficient 83
Covariant index 72

D

δ-method 25
Digital filter 33
Direct sum method 25